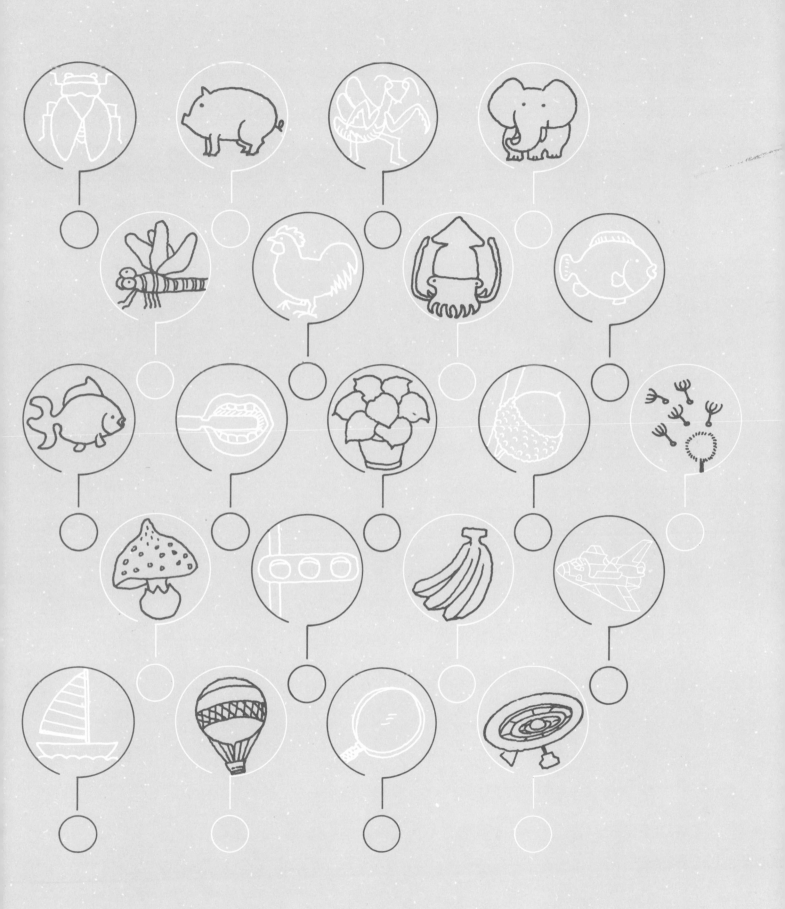

A Child's First Library of Learning

Famous Places

TIME-LIFE BOOKS • ALEXANDRIA, VIRGINIA

Contents

❓ Why Are There So Many Famous Places?

ANSWER If you could travel around the earth you would discover many wonderful things. You would see beautiful scenery and huge monuments built by people. Many places are so interesting that they are famous all over the world.

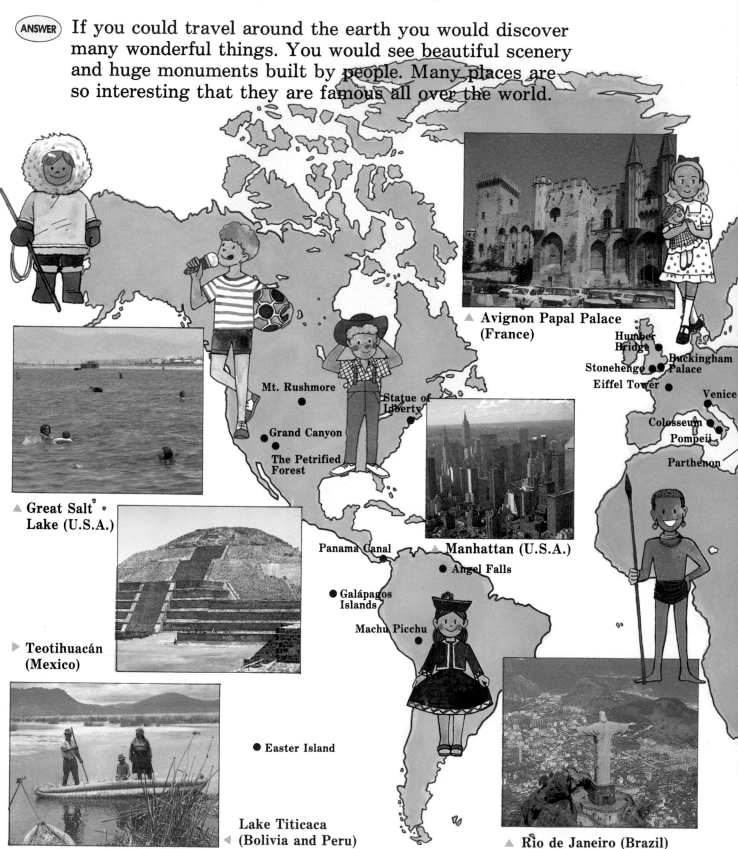

▲ Avignon Papal Palace (France)

Humber Bridge

Stonehenge

Buckingham Palace

Eiffel Tower

Venice

Colosseum

Pompeii

Parthenon

Mt. Rushmore

Statue of Liberty

Grand Canyon

The Petrified Forest

▲ Great Salt Lake (U.S.A.)

Panama Canal

▲ Manhattan (U.S.A.)

Angel Falls

Galápagos Islands

Machu Picchu

▶ Teotihuacán (Mexico)

● Easter Island

Lake Titicaca (Bolivia and Peru) ◀

▲ Rio de Janeiro (Brazil)

▼ Waterloo (Belgium)

▼ Petrodvorets Palace (U.S.S.R.)

● **To the Parent**

In this book your child will be introduced to some of the world's most famous places. Young children have trouble thinking about places beyond their home and community. Talk to your child about places he has seen on vacation. Remind him of postcards received from friends and family members. Use the maps in this book to help your child understand where different places are found.

Lake Baikal
(U.S.S.R.)

Kremlin

The
Great
Wall of
China

Seikan Tunnel

▲ The Forbidden City (China)

The Pyramids

Aswan Dam

Mohenjo-Daro
Taj Mahal (Pakistan)

Guilin

◀ Hong Kong Island

Himalayas
(Asia) ▼

The Great
Barrier Reef

Ayers Rock

Olga Mountains
(Australia) ▶

▲ Borobudur Temple
(Indonesia)

5

❓ Why Do Soldiers Stand on Guard At Buckingham Palace?

ANSWER Buckingham Palace is the home of the British Royal Family. Queen Elizabeth II lives there now. The soldiers who stand on guard at the palace have the job of protecting this important place from danger. A famous ceremony known as the Changing of the Guard takes place there at 11:30 a.m. daily. Tourists from all over the world come to see this colorful ceremony, during which new guards replace the ones on duty.

England

London

▶ **The palace guards**

Their red jackets and distinctive hats of black bear fur are famous sights.

▼ Buckingham Palace got its name from Lord Sheffield, one of the Dukes of Buckingham. Lord Sheffield was responsible for the palace's construction in 1703.

What Does the Flag Over Buckingham Palace Mean?

Sometimes a flag called the royal standard is seen flying over Buckingham Palace. When it is flying over the palace it means that Her Majesty the Queen is there. This is just a formal way of letting the people of Great Britain know that the Queen is at home.

What Are Some Other Famous Places in London?

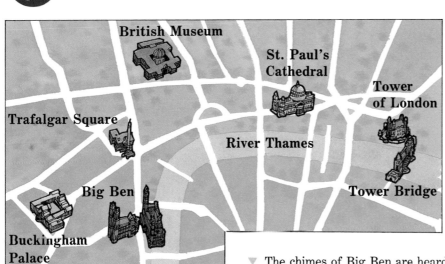

London is the capital of Britain. Many of its old buildings are important for historical or cultural reasons. The map shows where some of the famous ones are.

▼ **The Tower Bridge.** The middle span of this bridge can be raised to allow big ships to pass under it and continue to steam up or down the River Thames.

▼ The chimes of Big Ben are heard all over the city as they ring the time on each quarter-hour.

What Is It About This Bridge That Makes It So Famous?

ANSWER This is the Humber Bridge in England. It is the longest suspension bridge in the world. The bridge measures 4,626 feet (1,410 m) from one main support to the other. If all the wire used in the cables were laid in a straight line it would measure 44,000 miles (71,000 km), or almost long enough to go around the entire earth two times.

◀ The Humber Bridge is used by both cars and pedestrians.

Humber Bridge

London

■ How a suspension bridge is measured

The distance between the two main supports is the bridge's span.

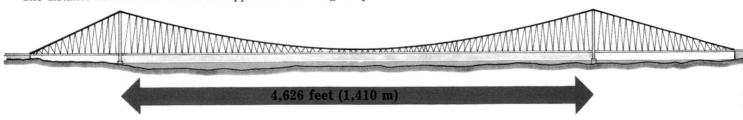

4,626 feet (1,410 m)

Different Types of Bridges

There are many types of bridges. People think of many things when building a bridge. They must know the kind of traffic that will pass over it and under it too.

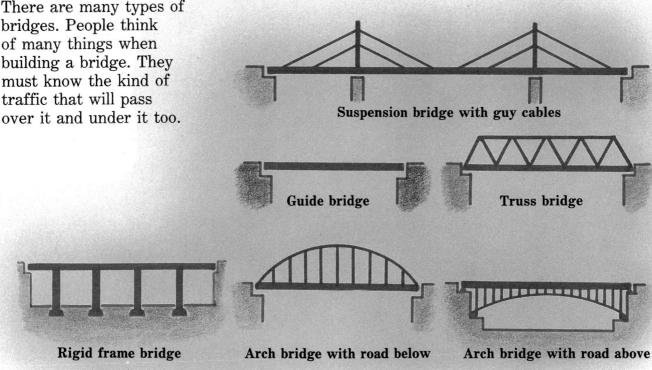

Suspension bridge with guy cables

Guide bridge

Truss bridge

Rigid frame bridge

Arch bridge with road below

Arch bridge with road above

Three unusual types of bridges

■ **Drawbridge.** The middle rises so that ships can pass beneath it.

■ **Lift bridge**

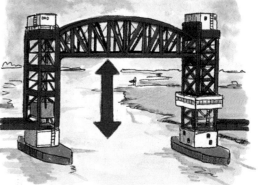

The bridge is raised to allow large ships to pass under it.

■ **Swing bridge.** It swings to the side to let big ships through.

❓ The Stonehenge Mystery: What Were These Huge Stones For?

ANSWER These giant stones at Stonehenge are about 3,500 years old. They are 16 to 30 feet (5 to 9 m) high and weigh 28 to 50 tons (25 to 45 t). We know they were built by ancient people, but why they were built is still quite a big mystery. Some people think that the rocks may have been placed to form a sort of calendar.

One way that Stonehenge might have

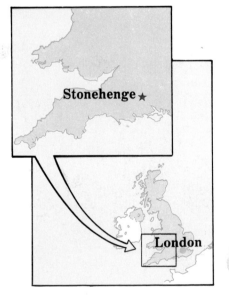

Stonehenge ★

London

First a trench was dug in the earth. One of its sides sloped at an angle. Then one of the big stones was slid into it.

A stone was lifted by logs as you see in the picture to the left. The job was then completed using ropes as you see in the picture above.

Was Stonehenge Used to Study the Sky?

One scientist used a computer to show that the stones may have been in positions to indicate the changes of season.

First a large circular trench was dug, and then dirt was piled on both sides of this trench.

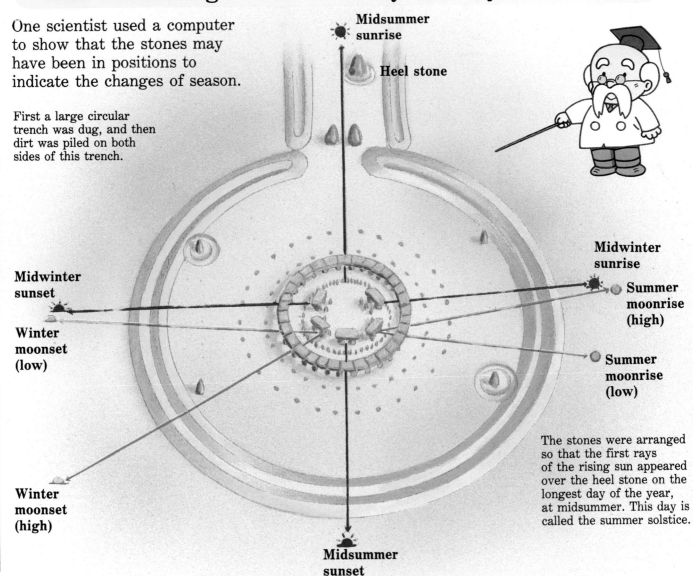

Midsummer sunrise

Heel stone

Midwinter sunset

Winter moonset (low)

Midwinter sunrise

Summer moonrise (high)

Summer moonrise (low)

Winter moonset (high)

Midsummer sunset

The stones were arranged so that the first rays of the rising sun appeared over the heel stone on the longest day of the year, at midsummer. This day is called the summer solstice.

been built

Wooden platforms were built. The stones were laid across them and slowly raised into position.

The cross-stone was raised one end at a time.

Finally the cross-stone was fitted into place on top of the other stones.

● To the Parent

The original layout, shown in the drawing above, consisted of an outer ditch and bank about 350 feet (107 m) across. Inside this were three rings, one of 60 holes and two of 30 holes each. Inside these was the circle of stones, about 100 feet (30 m) in diameter. Inside that was a circle of much smaller stones and holes and a U-shaped rock pattern surrounding an altar stone. It seems possible that it was used as a place of worship by an ancient people, but the sort of worship that may have been involved is not clear.

? **Why Was This Tower Built?**

ANSWER One hundred years ago a giant fair, or exposition, was to be held in Paris, France. To remember the event a tall tower was built. It was named after the man who built it, Gustave Eiffel. Today the Eiffel Tower is world famous. Every year millions of tourists go to a platform at the top. From there they enjoy a wonderful view of Paris.

▼ **Eiffel Tower**

Originally the Eiffel Tower was just 984 feet (300 m) high, but radio and TV transmitting antennas brought it to 1,053 feet (321 m). The tower was completed in the surprisingly short time of just 17 months.

● To the Parent

When people think of Paris today they invariably think of the Eiffel Tower. It is considered the very symbol of Paris. But when the tower was new in 1889 it was widely criticized. Many people felt that it was too modern for the traditional skyline of Paris.

What Are Some of the World's Tallest Structures?

Advances in technology allow us to erect taller and taller structures.

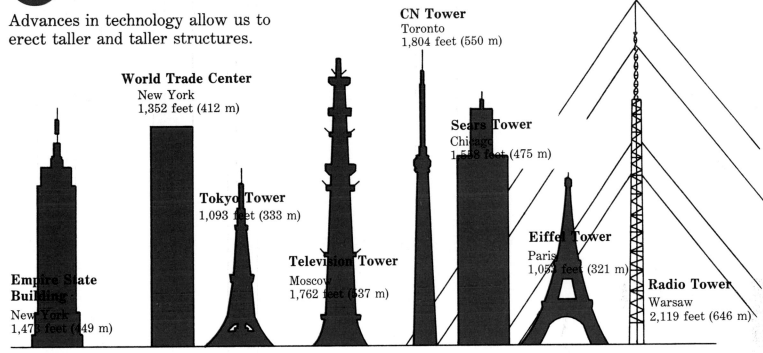

CN Tower
Toronto
1,804 feet (550 m)

World Trade Center
New York
1,352 feet (412 m)

Sears Tower
Chicago
1,558 feet (475 m)

Tokyo Tower
1,093 feet (333 m)

Television Tower
Moscow
1,762 feet (537 m)

Eiffel Tower
Paris
1,053 feet (321 m)

Empire State Building
New York
1,473 feet (449 m)

Radio Tower
Warsaw
2,119 feet (646 m)

There are many other famous places in Paris

Paris is the capital of France. The River Seine flows through the city. On the Right Bank are the Champs-Élysées, the Louvre Museum, the Élysée Palace and the Opera House. On the Left Bank are the student quarter and Montmartre. The Cathedral of Notre Dame stands on an island in the River Seine.

▲ **Arc de Triomphe.** Monument to Napoleon.

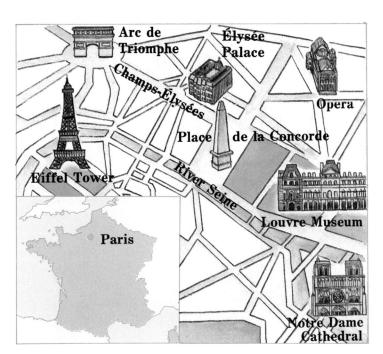

▲ **Paris Opera House.** Symbol of French culture.

Who Made the Palace of Versailles Such a Famous Place?

(ANSWER) It was a king of France, named Louis XIV, who turned this building into a magnificent palace. He filled its rooms with beautiful furniture and decorations. The area around the palace was turned into lovely gardens with many sculptures and fountains. Today France is no longer ruled by a king, but this old palace is still very famous.

▶ **Louis XIV's Bedroom**
The walls of the king's bedroom were decorated with a design in real gold.

▼ **Outside.** The beautiful parks and gardens that surround the royal palace at Versailles were carefully planned. In the center is a statue that shows King Louis XIV mounted on his horse.

Chapel. The floor of the room is covered in beautiful designs in marble. Louis XVI and Marie Antoinette were married in this chapel in 1770, four years before he became king.

The Queen's Salon

This is the room where the queen met her guests. Here she welcomed foreign visitors and French royalty.

▼ Battle Room

This room celebrates the victories of the king's armies. A sculpture on the wall shows the king riding his horse into a battle.

Peace Room. How different from the king's Battle Room! It was used by France's queens as a music room or as a private place in which to read or quietly pass the time.

Hall of Mirrors. An enormous and splendid gallery, it features 17 windows overlooking the gardens. On the opposite side there are 17 false windows. These are made of more than 500 mirrored panes.

15

❓ What Is So Unusual About These Cave Paintings?

(ANSWER) These paintings, in a cave at Lascaux, France, were drawn by Stone Age people called Cro-Magnons. They lived 25,000 years ago. On the cave walls are about 100 drawings of various animals, one of them an oxlike beast called an aurochs. Some of the paintings are 20 feet (6 m) high, and many of them show that the artists had remarkable skill.

▼ The Lascaux paintings are very lifelike.

◀ **Man and animals**
Outside the caves ▶

16

■ How were they done?

The cave dwellers used colored clays and charcoal, and painted the pictures with their fingers. For lighting they used stone lamps with animal fat as fuel.

■ How were they found?

Four young boys lost their dog while they were out playing in a field. They thought he might have fallen into a small hole they discovered in the grass. They dug at the hole and made it big enough so they could squeeze through.

Inside they were amazed at what they found. They were in a big cave. But not just an ordinary cave. Its walls were covered with marvelous pictures. And they found their dog too. They made their discovery about 50 years ago.

Paintings at Altamira in Spain

Caves at Altamira also contain many paintings. In an area that extends from southwest France to northern Spain there are a great many caverns that have ancient wall paintings and also some sculptures. When the first ones were found, no one believed the paintings were that old. Since then studies have shown that these pictures are ancient works of art.

Altamira scene ▶

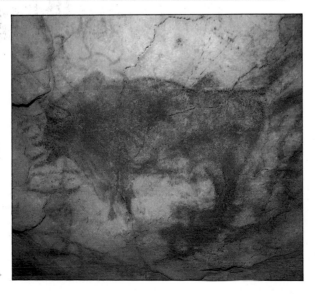

● To the Parent

The Lascaux cave's drawings of horses, deer and bison, which had been the cave dwellers' main source of food, became a major tourist attraction. But that brought pollution. By the early 1960s scientists noticed algae on some paintings. They decided that they had been caused by the humidity of exhaled breath in the cave. In 1963 the cave was closed to avoid further damage to the paintings. But in another cave, which was named Lascaux 2, scientifically exact replicas of the cave art were drawn, and Lascaux 2 is open every day of the year except Tuesdays, when all French museums are closed, and during January, when there are simply too few visitors to that historic region of France.

Why Is Venice Called the City of Canals?

ANSWER Venice is a famous city in Italy. It was built long ago on 118 small islands. The parts of the city are connected by canals. To get from one section of Venice to another you usually take a boat. The islands are also connected by more than 400 bridges. This unusual city is a very popular tourist attraction.

Venice

Italy

Rome

▶ Gondolas

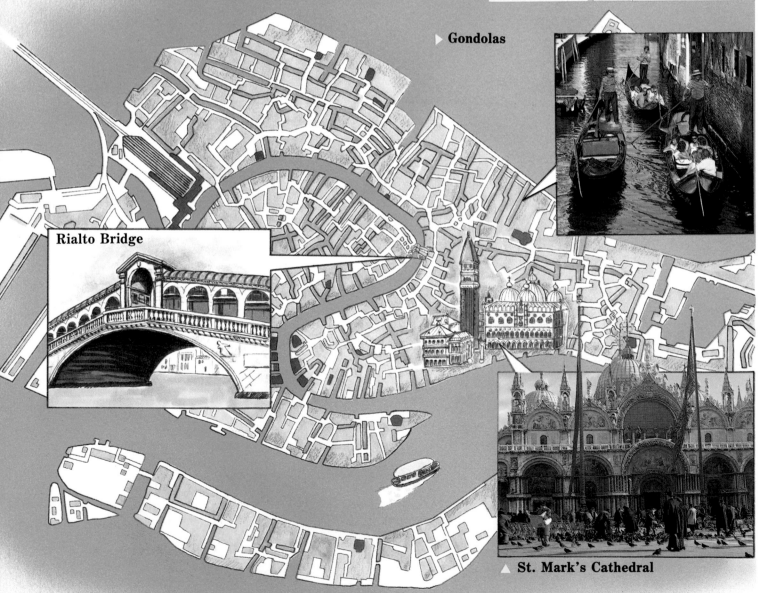

Rialto Bridge

▲ St. Mark's Cathedral

■ The gondolas of Venice

Boats called gondolas are used by many visitors who come to Venice. But the people who live here use canal buses or motorboats much the way people in other cities use cars. Private motorboats are tied in front of the houses.

◀ Gondolas glide along one of the big canals.

● **To the Parent**

People began to settle in Venice about the middle of the 5th Century. These were the Venetos, who migrated here from the shores of the Adriatic Sea. Venice was a muddy, swampy area at that time, but it flourished and became an important trade gateway. As it prospered it also became a center for the arts. Today Venice has serious problems caused by air and water pollution. It is causing damage to the city's beautiful marble buildings. And Venice is slowly sinking into the sea. It will take a great deal of ingenuity to save this city and its many treasures from the sea and the ravages of pollution.

Where Do the Automobiles Drive?

They don't use automobiles in Venice. The few streets the city has are too narrow and twisting for driving. Bicycles are not much use either. Venice has a great many bridges that people use to get across canals. There are so many steps at the bridges that bicycles are not very practical.

So boats are really the most practical way to get around in Venice. The canal system is as developed as the road networks in other cities. People go to work or shopping or to the movies by taking a motorboat or one of the canal buses. To them this way of traveling seems ordinary.

19

❓ Why Does the Tower of Pisa Lean?

▲ The marble tower is 184 feet (56 m) high.

ANSWER

This is one of the world's most famous buildings. It was built hundreds of years ago. After the first three stories were finished the ground below it began to sink. That caused the tower to lean. Engineers who measure it say the tower leans a bit more all the time. Every 20 years it leans another inch (2½ cm). People hope they will keep the tower from falling over.

Oh oh! It looks like it's going to fall over! I hope it doesn't land on me.

■ How much does it lean?

Right now the tower is about 17 feet (5½ m) out of line. If you stood at the top and dropped a stone it would land about 17 feet from the base of the tower. People have measured the tower every year since 1911. That's how they know it leans more and more all the time.

■ It's level on top

Only the bell tower at the top does not lean. That's because it was added later.

Galileo and the tower

Galileo Galilei was a scientist who was born in Pisa in 1564. Legend says that Galileo dropped two balls, one 100 times as heavy as the other, together from the top of the tower to show that both would hit the ground at the same time. Whether he did this or not, Galileo's careful experiments did show that objects of different weights fall at the same speed if the effects of air resistance are discounted. It is also said that he discovered the principle of a pendulum's swing by watching swaying chandeliers in the tower.

● **To the Parent**

The science of dynamics had made very little, if any, progress from Aristotle's time until Galileo's. It was thought that if two objects, one 10 times as heavy as the other, were dropped together the lighter would take 10 times as long to hit the ground. It wasn't known that objects with lighter density get lift from the resistance of the air below them, while heavier objects do not. The credit for proving the point went to Galileo, although similar experiments had been conducted in Holland during Galileo's time by a Dutch physicist named Simon Stevin.

![] How Old Is the Roman Colosseum?

ANSWER It was built nearly 2,000 years ago. Much of this stadium still stands in Rome, Italy. In ancient times people came here to watch special ceremonies and events.

▲ The outside of the Colosseum

■ Inside the ruins

The Colosseum was one of the most famous buildings of ancient Rome. It is proof that the Romans were skillful builders. This huge building is oval in shape. It is approximately 660 feet (201 m) long and 560 feet (171 m) wide and rises to a height of 160 feet (49 m). Its four levels could hold more than 48,000 people.

■ Here men fought wild beasts

The ancient Romans came to the Colosseum to watch men fight with wild animals. At the opening ceremonies about 80 A.D. fights were held for 100 days. Huge numbers of men and animals lost their lives.

Some of the special features of the Colosseum

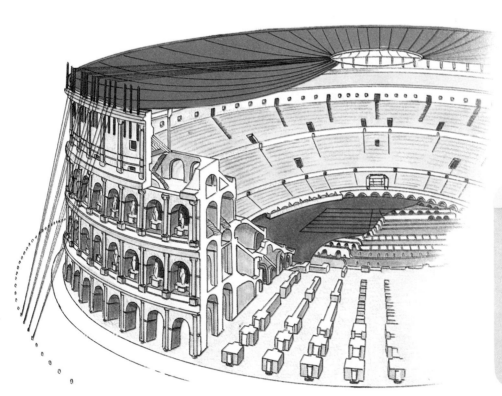

Canvas tents were built to protect the people from sun or rain while they watched the battles. The center of the arena was designed so it could be flooded and water battles were held. Two-level corridors led from outside the Colosseum to the seats so that crowds of people could get into the arena quickly.

● To the Parent

The Colosseum remained in use up to about 500 A.D. Part of it was demolished by an earthquake in the Middle Ages. Later some of the marble was cut away and used to build churches. The seats have crumbled away, and the arena is in a very bad state of disrepair. Still it stands as a monumental testimonial to the creative genius of the ancient Romans. It is one of many grand monuments of Rome that now are tourist attractions.

23

❓ Why Is the Old City Of Pompeii So Famous?

ANSWER Pompeii was a large city in ancient Italy. There were many shops in this busy town. Pompeii was located near the volcano called Mt. Vesuvius. Just over 1,900 years ago the volcano erupted and destroyed the city. In modern times people discovered the city buried under 25 feet (8 m) of ash. It showed them how people lived in ancient Rome.

▼ Main street

Pompeii's roads were orderly and paved. A wall surrounded the city. Public facilities were modern for that age, 2,000 or more years ago.

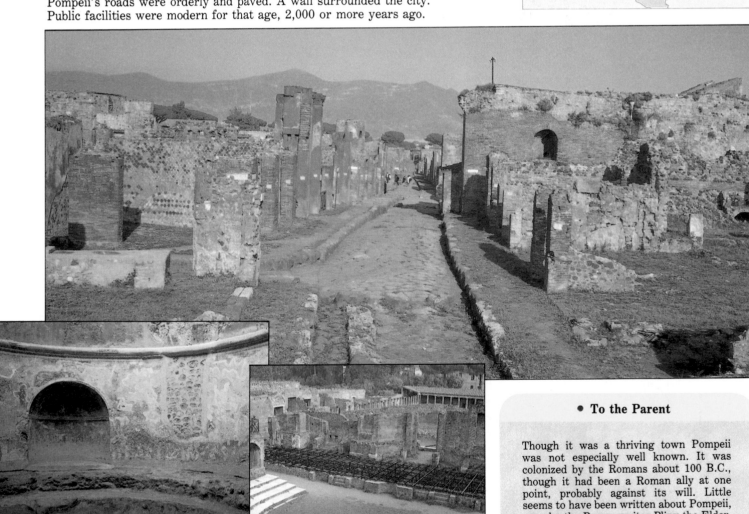

▲ **Public baths**

Amphitheater ▶

● **To the Parent**

Though it was a thriving town Pompeii was not especially well known. It was colonized by the Romans about 100 B.C., though it had been a Roman ally at one point, probably against its will. Little seems to have been written about Pompeii, even by the Roman writer Pliny the Elder, who was killed trying to rescue friends at Stabiae during the eruption. An isolated villa named Oplontis, also buried by the volcano, was not discovered until 1964.

24

The city of Pompeii

The city's streets were orderly. There were public baths and amphitheaters. Each house had its own water supply.

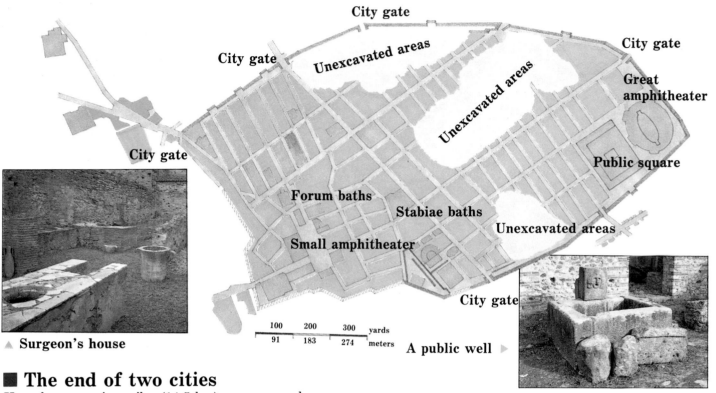

▲ Surgeon's house

City gate

City gate

City gate

City gate

City gate

City gate

Unexcavated areas

Unexcavated areas

Unexcavated areas

Great amphitheater

Public square

Forum baths

Stabiae baths

Small amphitheater

| 100 | 200 | 300 | yards |
| 91 | 183 | 274 | meters |

A public well ▶

The end of two cities

Herculaneum, nine miles (14.5 km) away, was also buried. An earthquake hit both cities in 62 A.D., and they had not recovered when Vesuvius erupted.

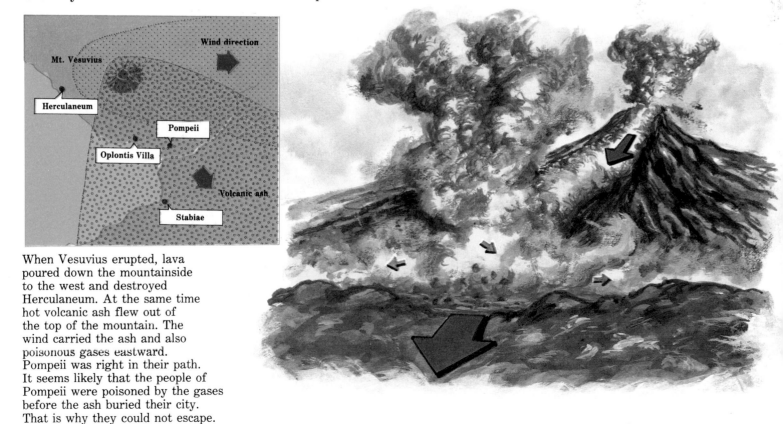

Wind direction

Mt. Vesuvius

Herculaneum

Pompeii

Oplontis Villa

Volcanic ash

Stabiae

When Vesuvius erupted, lava poured down the mountainside to the west and destroyed Herculaneum. At the same time hot volcanic ash flew out of the top of the mountain. The wind carried the ash and also poisonous gases eastward. Pompeii was right in their path. It seems likely that the people of Pompeii were poisoned by the gases before the ash buried their city. That is why they could not escape.

What Is the World's Smallest Country?

ANSWER The Vatican is the smallest country in the world. The entire country is just over a sixth of a square mile (.44 km²) in size. Only 1,500 people live there. The Vatican is located in the center of Rome. It has been an independent country for more than 60 years.

Italy

Vatican City

◀ Crowds gather in St. Peter's Square.

▼ Here is the square seen from the air.

■ How big is it?

The Vatican is about the same size as 60 soccer fields put together.

60

■ Numerous facilities

In addition to St. Peter's Basilica, the most
impressive Catholic church in the world, and
St. Peter's Square the
Vatican has its own
museum, a broadcasting
station, newspaper offices
and a railway station.
Although an independent
country it is easily
entered from Rome.

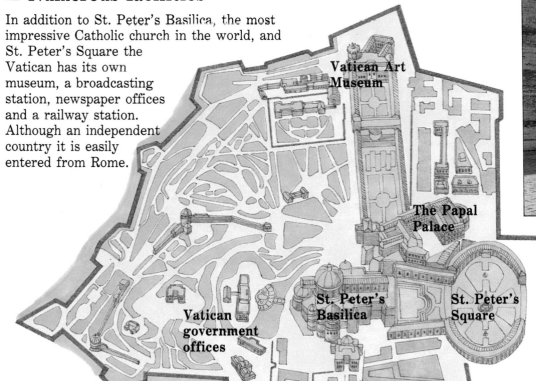

Vatican Art Museum

The Papal Palace

Vatican government offices

St. Peter's Basilica

St. Peter's Square

The Vatican is guarded by a
corps of soldiers known as
the Swiss Guards. Their
brightly colored uniforms
were designed by the great
Italian artist Michelangelo,
whose paintings decorate
many of the buildings here.

The five smallest countries

Despite their size these small countries each have special
features that make some of them popular tourist attractions.

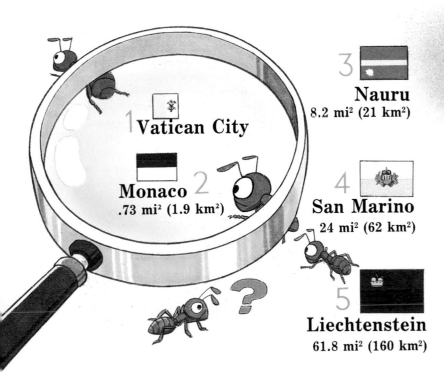

1 Vatican City

Monaco 2
.73 mi² (1.9 km²)

3 Nauru
8.2 mi² (21 km²)

4 San Marino
24 mi² (62 km²)

5 Liechtenstein
61.8 mi² (160 km²)

If all these five tiny
independent countries were
put together their total
land area wouldn't cover an
area even one ninth the
size of the city of London.

Why Did the Greeks Build the Parthenon?

(ANSWER) The Parthenon was built 2,400 years ago. The Greeks constructed this temple to honor the goddess Athena. It was believed that she protected the city of Athens from harm. Today the ruins of the Parthenon are still standing.

▼ **The Parthenon**

The goddess Athena

The ancient Greeks believed she was a goddess with special powers to protect the city of Athens from harm. When the Parthenon was built on the Acropolis, a fortified hill overlooking the city, a large statue of her stood at its center.

The Pride of Athens

Ancient Greece was made up of a number of different city-states. The greatest of these was Athens, which was built around a tall hill called the Acropolis. The dominant feature on the Acropolis was the temple dedicated to Athena.

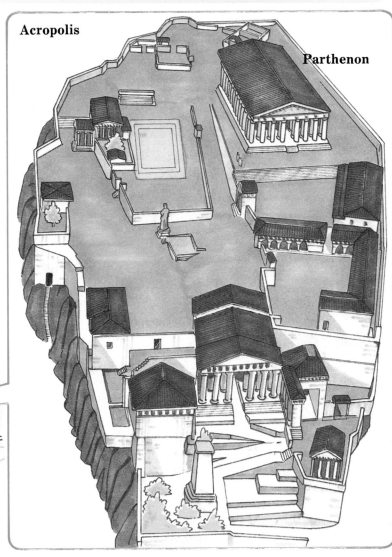

Acropolis

Parthenon

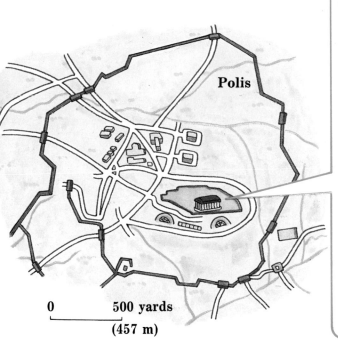

Polis

0   500 yards

(457 m)

 ## How Did They Build Those Tall Columns?

The Parthenon is famous for its huge columns. They rise to a height of 32 feet (10 m). Each column is made from a number of round stones. They were piled one on top of the other. Wood or metal wedges were placed in the center to keep them in place.

Do You Know What a Fjord Is?

(ANSWER) Fjords are long, narrow bodies of water. They are formed by glaciers. These rivers of moving ice cut deep valleys in the mountains. When the ice melts the sea moves in and fills them with water. Norway is famous for its beautiful fjords.

Norway
Oslo
Sweden
Stockholm
Gulf of Bothnia
Finland
Helsinki

Geiranger Fjord, Norway ▶

■ How fjords are made

The mountains are entirely covered by glaciers.

The glaciers start moving slowly down the valleys.

 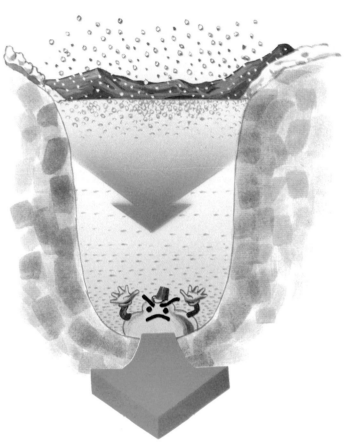

And What Causes These Glaciers?

High mountains and cold places like the Arctic and Antarctic are covered by snow all year. The snow never melts. As more snow falls on top of the snow that has already settled, layers upon layers pile up. As this happens the snow at the bottom is crushed into ice and forms glaciers. Glaciers are huge rivers of ice that slide slowly down the mountainsides.

Over thousands of years the moving glaciers wear valley walls. The sea rushes in and fills the valleys.

● **To the Parent**

Fjords are common geological features along the coasts of Scandinavia. They are long, narrow and deep inlets enclosed on either side by sheer, high cliffs. Fjords are formed by glacial erosion. Glaciers that are the accumulation of tens of thousands of years of snowfall in the mountains are called valley glaciers. Glaciers that form on level surfaces, like those in the polar ice, are called continental glaciers. These rivers of ice move at a speed of from an inch (2-3 cm) to 3 or 4 feet (1.2 m) a day. Their force is vastly greater than that of any river, and they easily slice away the sides of valleys as they move through them. Glacial erosion formed many of the natural scenic wonders found in the world.

What Kind of Place Is the Kremlin?

ANSWER The Kremlin is located on a hill in the city of Moscow, the capital of the Soviet Union. It is the center of the government of Russia. Inside the Kremlin are many government buildings. They are protected by a wall built around them. The word kremlin means fortress in Russian. Visitors to this famous place also see theaters, museums and monuments.

▼ **Cathedral of the Annunciation**

▼ **Great Kremlin Palace**

1. Cathedral of the Annunciation 2. Great Kremlin Palace 3. Red Square 4. State of St. Basil 6. Lenin's Tomb 7. Redeemer Tower 8. Council of Ministers Building 11. Cathedral of the Assumption 12. Armory 13. Palace of Congresses 14. Arsenal

▲ Red Square

Arctic Ocean

U.S.S.R.

Moscow

Caspian Sea

Historical Museum 5. Cathedral
. Tsar Cannon 10. Tsar Bell
5. GUM Department Store

▲ State Historical Museum

▲ Cathedral of St. Basil

■ Tsar Bell and Tsar Cannon

This bell weighs 200 tons (180 t), and the cannon weighs 43 tons (38 t). They were never used.

Ugh! It's heavy!

So is this!

●To the Parent

Citadels known as kremlins were built in the center of many Russian cities during the Middle Ages. Many survive today in cities across the U.S.S.R., but the best known is the Kremlin in Moscow. Russia's government, the Supreme Soviet, is housed in the Great Kremlin Palace. Although many people believe that it's impossible to get inside the Kremlin, the fact is that many tourists visit it every day. Artifacts from the tsarist era are on display there.

Why Is the Statue of Liberty In New York Harbor?

(ANSWER) The Statue of Liberty is a symbol of freedom and one of friendship too. The statue was a gift to the United States. It was given to our country by the people of France. It was their way of remembering the support they gave the United States during its war for independence. The statue has been standing in New York Harbor since 1886.

▼ Miss Liberty, soaring 302 feet (92 m) above the harbor, has greeted visitors to America's shores for more than 100 years.

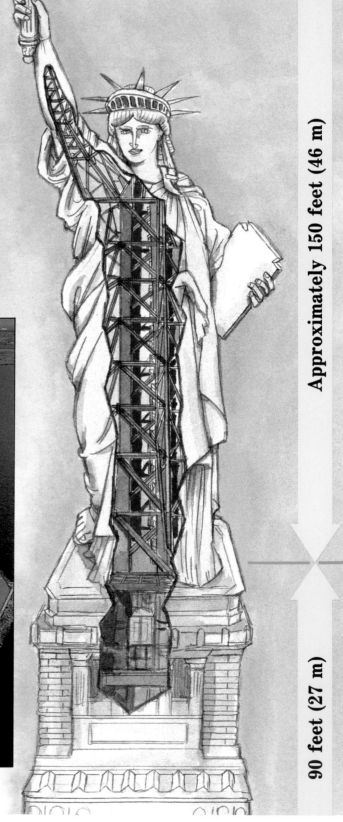

Approximately 150 feet (46 m)

90 feet (27 m)

The Statue Was Designed and Built in France

The Statue of Liberty celebrates the friendship and aid that France gave America when that country was fighting for its independence from Britain in the 1770s. Only France sent troops to help. The drawings show how the statue was assembled.

▲ Sculptor Frédéric Bartholdi started with a small clay model. Then he built a bigger one.

▼ Next came a model that was one quarter of full size. This was used to make the finished statue.

▼ Using the model the statue was cast in copper.

▲ The head was the final piece.

▼ The finished statue, weighing 225 tons (200 t), was shipped in sections to New York on a French ship. It took several years to assemble.

▶ Supported by a steel frame to prevent warping, the copper sections were fitted back together and placed on a stand that the Americans had built.

● To the Parent

In the century since its dedication the statue had become the symbol of America, and it had also deteriorated badly. With public donations it was refurbished, and on its centennial Chief Justice Warren E. Burger swore in 5,000 new Americans on Liberty Island, while all across the land 20,000 other new citizens were sworn in simultaneously in a satellite telecast.

What Kind of Places Become National Parks?

ANSWER Some of the most famous places in our country are national parks. These places have been set aside for all of us to enjoy. Many have beautiful scenery. Some help us remember important moments in our history.

▲ **Yosemite: California.** Visitors here see Yosemite Falls. It's the second highest waterfall in the world. There are giant redwood trees that are many centuries old.

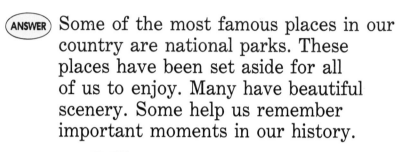

▲ **Sequoia: California.** Here are the giant sequoias, which are a species of redwood and are among the world's oldest and largest living things. Many are 3,000 to 4,000 years old, and some have a diameter of more than 30 feet (9 m).

■ National treasures

The national parks of America are scattered from Alaska to Hawaii and the American Virgin Islands. The United States Congress decides which areas will be chosen as national parks. At present there are about 50. Millions of people get pleasure from these parks, and they are great national treasures.

Yellowstone: Wyoming, Montana and Idaho

This was America's first national park and is its largest. It has 10,000 geysers, including the famous Old Faithful. It is rich in wildlife, lakes and waterfalls. But in 1988 forest fires destroyed thousands of acres of woodland, and it could be many years before new timber can grow back.

Mesa Verde: Colorado

This park was established in 1906 to save important cliff dwellings. They were home to the Pueblo Indians long before Columbus made his voyage to America. The park is noted for its rugged scenery.

Everglades National Park

●● 3

▲ **Everglades: Florida.** This park is a huge marsh. It stretches in a broad strip across south Florida. The Everglades is famous for its plants and wildlife. Many endangered animals, including crocodiles, alligators and bald eagles, live there.

1 Acadia	17 Grand Canyon
2 Shenandoah	18 Zion
3 Biscayne	19 Bryce Canyon
4 Great Smoky Mountains	20 Capitol Reef
5 Hot Springs	21 Canyonlands
6 Mammoth Cave	22 Arches
7 Isle Royale	23 Grand Teton
8 Voyageurs	24 Glacier
9 Theodore Roosevelt	25 Mt. Revelstoke, Canada
10 Wind Cave	26 North Cascades
11 Badlands	27 Olympic
12 Rocky Mountains	28 Mt. Rainier
13 Carlsbad Caverns	29 Crater Lake
14 Guadalupe Mountains	30 Redwood
15 Big Bend	31 Lassen Volcanic
16 Petrified Forest	32 Kings Canyon
	33 Channel Islands

● To the Parent

America's national parks are vast. Yellowstone National Park alone is almost twice as large as the state of Delaware. It is impossible to cover most of them by foot. To see the sights visitors usually travel by car or bus, or in some cases by airplane or helicopter. Notices and directional signs in the parks use international symbols as well as English to make it easy for visitors from foreign lands to find their way around.

? How Was the Grand Canyon Formed?

ANSWER The Grand Canyon in Arizona is more than 200 miles (322 km) long and 5,300 feet (1,615 m) deep in some places. This huge canyon was formed by water erosion. The Colorado River wore away the sides of the canyon. It took millions of years for this to happen. It is still happening today.

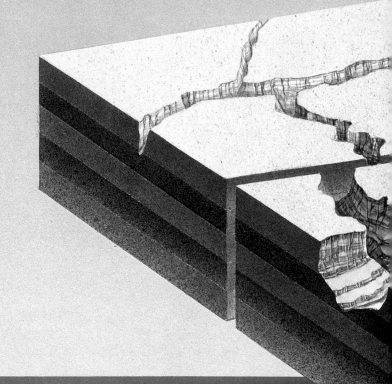

▼ The Grand Canyon

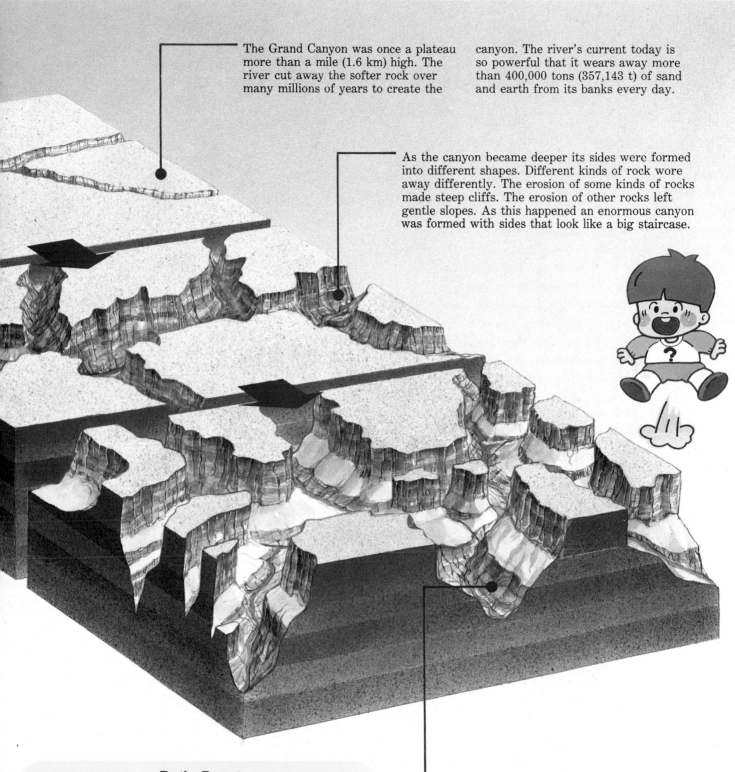

The Grand Canyon was once a plateau more than a mile (1.6 km) high. The river cut away the softer rock over many millions of years to create the canyon. The river's current today is so powerful that it wears away more than 400,000 tons (357,143 t) of sand and earth from its banks every day.

As the canyon became deeper its sides were formed into different shapes. Different kinds of rock wore away differently. The erosion of some kinds of rocks made steep cliffs. The erosion of other rocks left gentle slopes. As this happened an enormous canyon was formed with sides that look like a big staircase.

● **To the Parent**

The Grand Canyon is an area of magnificent scenery and is perhaps the best known of all of America's national parks. The canyon itself is a massive gorge. Visitors follow trails from the top down into the canyon, usually by mule trains. Fossils revealed in layers of exposed rock strata along the sides of the canyon include conifer needles, dragonflies, and even sharks, which offer positive evidence that this area has alternated between being seabed and mountaintop. The Grand Canyon is a shining example of the breathtaking artistry in nature and reveals some ways that nature works.

The Grand Canyon is made of many layers of rock. By studying the sides of the canyon, people have learned a great deal about the land. Scientists who study rocks have discovered fossils in the canyon's walls. At the bottom of the canyon walls are fossils of ocean life. These are about 570 million years old. Higher up on the walls they found fossils of a certain kind of fern. These are 280 million years old. The walls of the canyon are a museum of the earth's history.

？ Whose Faces Are Carved In Mount Rushmore?

(ANSWER) The faces of four of America's greatest Presidents can be seen at Mount Rushmore. They are George Washington, Thomas Jefferson, Abraham Lincoln and Theodore Roosevelt. This national monument is located in South Dakota. Every year more than one million tourists come to see it.

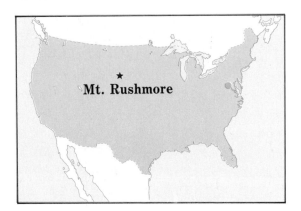

★ Mt. Rushmore

National memorial ▶

The four Presidents (left to right) are George Washington, Thomas Jefferson, Theodore Roosevelt and Abraham Lincoln.

？ What Did Each of These Four Presidents Achieve?

George Washington (1732-1799)

He led the American people to victory in the American Revolution. He helped draft the Constitution of the new nation and was elected the first President.

Thomas Jefferson (1743-1826)

He was the author of the Declaration of Independence. A wealthy farmer, he studied law and served in Congress before he was elected President in 1800.

40

■ Monumental

The head of Washington is about 60 feet (18 m) high. Made to the same scale a complete statue of the first President would be about 465 feet (142 m) high.

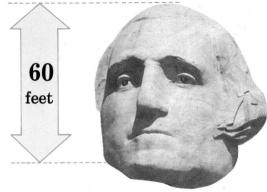

60 feet

Abraham Lincoln (1809-1865)

Lincoln's election on an antislavery platform in 1860 led to the secession of 11 Southern states. He took the nation to war in 1861 to preserve the Union.

Theodore Roosevelt (1858-1919)

He was a conservationist and also supported progressive laws designed to help the little man. He also ruled out non-American intervention in Latin-American affairs.

❓ What Caused The Petrified Forest?

ANSWER Millions of years ago much of Arizona was covered with forest. Over time trees fell and were buried under dirt and sand. As more time passed, a natural process turned the buried trees to stone. When this happens to something it is said to be petrified. When wind and water blew away the loose dirt around them, petrified trees could be seen covering the ground.

▶ These petrified trees lived millions of years ago. Now they are stone.

How nature turns trees into stone

About 200 million years ago the land around eastern Arizona looked very different. It was covered by a large jungle. There were ferns, pine and cedar trees.

When the trees died they fell to the ground. They were swept away by a great flood. The trees landed in low places in the ground. They were covered with dirt and sand.

Petrified Forest National Park

★

● **To the Parent**

The Petrified Forest is in a corner of an area called the Painted Desert. It is believed that the trees were fossilized because of the swampy soil where they were buried. It retarded decay and allowed time for the trees to petrify. The process replaces the natural wood fibers with silica. The process is often so accurate that the structure of the tree, inside and out, is just like the original.

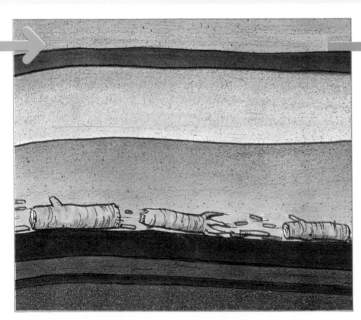

A thick layer of dirt and sand covered the trees. As they decayed, the trees were protected by the soil. They slowly turned into fossils that were as hard as stone.

Over millions of years the soil that covered the trees was washed away by rain. The petrified trees were left lying on the surface. They can still be seen today.

How Can Big Ships Get Through the Panama Canal?

ANSWER This canal connects the Atlantic and Pacific Oceans. It has a series of giant water tanks, which are called locks. When a ship enters a lock, water is added. The ship rises with the water. Locks can connect two bodies of water that are at different heights. Ships in the canal are raised so that they can go across Gatun Lake. It is found in the center of the canal.

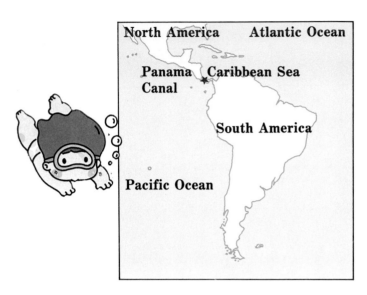

▲ An oceangoing cargo ship enters the canal.

Enlarged plan of Gatun

Ships entering the canal from the Caribbean Sea on the Atlantic Ocean side enter lock A, and the gates are closed. The water level inside is the same as sea level. Lock B is higher than sea level, so water gate A is opened and water from lock B pours into lock A. This makes the water level in both locks equal and raises the ship.

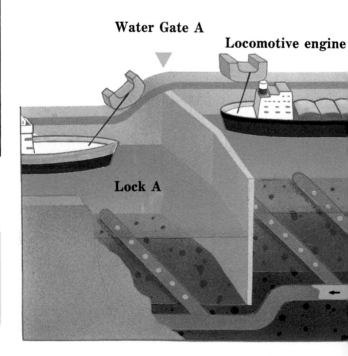

Water Gate A

Locomotive engine

Lock A

● **To the Parent**

While the Panama Canal has locks the Suez Canal has none since it is at the same level as the sea along its 100-mile (160 km) length. Canals can greatly shorten shipping routes. The Suez Canal trims 5,500 miles (8,900 km) off the distance between London and India. The Panama Canal cuts the distance between Pacific Ocean ports and the Caribbean by 8,100 miles (13,000 km).

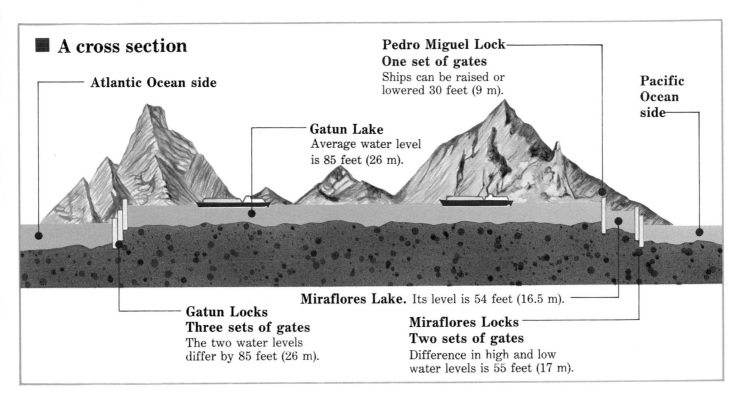

■ A cross section

Atlantic Ocean side

**Pedro Miguel Lock—
One set of gates**
Ships can be raised or
lowered 30 feet (9 m).

**Pacific
Ocean
side—**

Gatun Lake
Average water level
is 85 feet (26 m).

Miraflores Lake. Its level is 54 feet (16.5 m). —

**Gatun Locks
Three sets of gates**
The two water levels
differ by 85 feet (26 m).

**Miraflores Locks
Two sets of gates**
Difference in high and low
water levels is 55 feet (17 m).

Locks

2 When the ship reaches the far side of lock B
water gate B is opened. The water level
and the ship in lock B are both raised to
the same height as the water level of lock C.

3 Finally gate C is opened and the water and
the ship in lock C are raised to the same level
as the water in Gatun Lake. The ship can then
proceed across the lake. Because of the time
spent passing through the lock system it takes
a ship about eight hours to go through the canal.

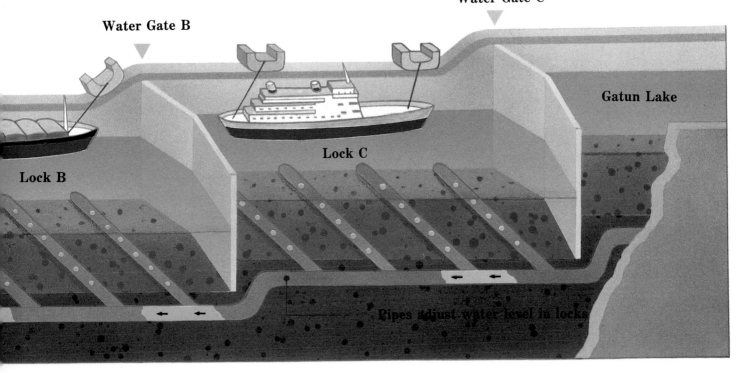

Water Gate C

Water Gate B

Gatun Lake

Lock C

Lock B

Pipes adjust water level in locks

What Waterfall Is the Highest?

(ANSWER) The tallest waterfall is in South America. Angel Falls on the upper Caroni River in Venezuela drops 3,212 feet (979 m). The falls are in an area of thick tropical rain forest. They are named after James A. Angel, an American pilot. He had to make a forced landing in his plane there in 1937 and discovered them by chance.

■ The waterfall makes a spectacular drop in stages from the Plateau of Guyana. Its highest single fall is 2,648 feet (807 m).

3,212 feet (979 m)

● **To the Parent**

Niagara Falls has two precipices, the higher of which is only 167 feet (51 m). But it is famous because it is on the border between the United States and Canada and is easy to reach, and a great volume of water rushes over the falls. On the other hand Angel Falls, which is almost 20 times as high as Niagara, gets few visitors because it takes a five-day boat trip to reach it.

■ How are waterfalls made?

1. Flowing lava from a volcano may block the upper waters of a river or a stream and cause a lake to be formed. Eventually the water from the lake will overflow this natural dam, and this creates a waterfall.

2. A fast-flowing river may severely wear away and deepen its riverbed. A slower-moving branch, unable to maintain the same rate of erosion, will form a waterfall at the point where it flows into the main river.

3. Part of a riverbed may be formed of hard rock that does not wear away as quickly as surrounding soft rock. The flowing water of the river cuts away the softer rock at a faster rate, and a waterfall is created.

Did you know that a waterfall can move?

The force of the water flowing over Niagara Falls is so great that it wears away the base rock. The result is that the falls are moving farther up the river at two to three feet (.6 to .9 m) every year.

◀ Sightseeing boats at Niagara Falls

▼ Movement of Niagara Falls

American side

Canadian side

2,000 years ago ▶

◀ 4,000 years ago

12,000 years ago ◀

About 6 miles (9.6 km)

■ How a waterfall erodes rock

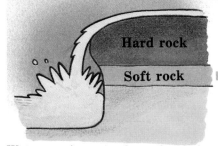

Hard rock

Soft rock

Water pouring over the rock splashes violently against the softer rock closer to the bottom of the falls.

The water striking the lower rock gradually wears it away. This action may continue for millions of years.

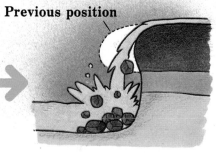

Previous position

With the lower rock eroded away the hard upper rock has no support and crumbles under the water's weight.

47

?Did You Know That There's a Place Called the Lost City of the Andes?

ANSWER This ancient city is located high in the Andes Mountains in the modern country of Peru. It was built by the Incas. These South American Indians are famous for their skill as builders.

■ Plan of Machu Picchu

It was a very orderly city, with a temple and a main square.

1. Lookout post
2. Terraced fields
3. Water supply
4. Queen's palace
5. King's palace
6. Sacred temple
7. Worship stone
8. Main gate

▲ This temple was dedicated to the queen and the sun.

■ The empire ruled by the Incas

The Incas had a mighty empire long before Christopher Columbus and others came to the New World. They lived in much of South America. The center of their world was the city of Cuzco. It is located in Peru.

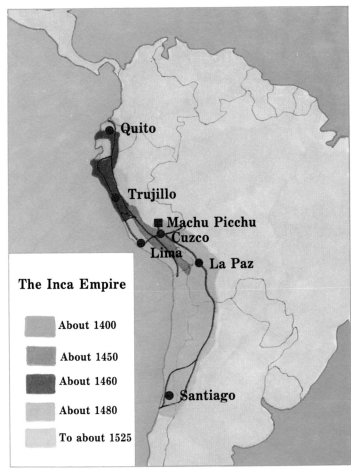

Quito

Trujillo

Machu Picchu
Cuzco
Lima
La Paz

The Inca Empire

About 1400

About 1450

About 1460

About 1480

To about 1525

Santiago

▲ These are ruins of homes where ordinary people lived.

Incan culture: the two extremes

The Incas were very talented people and excellent builders. But they had no written language so some things about them remain a mystery.

▲ Many roads were lined by walls.

A quipu carried a message.

▲ They tied knots to send messages.

● **To the Parent**

Machu Picchu is a major historical relic in almost perfect condition. There are various theories about Machu Picchu: that it was a main fortified base of the Inca Empire for the region of the Amazon; or that it was a city built for religious purposes; or that it was a secret city and its true purpose has yet to be discovered. Little remains to help us clear up the mysteries surrounding Incan culture. There is not even anyone living today who can interpret the meaning of the quipu.

? What Are the Galápagos Islands Most Famous For?

ANSWER These islands are located in the Pacific Ocean. They are far away from any other land. Their name comes from a Spanish word that means tortoise. The Galápagos Islands are most famous for the unusual animals that live there. If you could visit the islands you would see wildlife unlike that anywhere else in the world.

Equator
★ Quito
Ecuador

Pacific Ocean

▶ **A frigate bird.** The male has a red crop, or pouch, on his neck. The female does not.

▼ **Land iguana.** This big lizard lives on the fleshy leaves of the cactus plant. It lies in the sun and has no apparent fear of people.

▲ **Giant tortoise.** It is said that some of these big turtles grow to weigh as much as 500 to 600 pounds (225-275 kg).

Galápagos Islands

Equator

Isabela Island

■ The Galápagos Islands

Although they are located on the equator the Galápagos are washed by cold sea currents. Fresh water is scarce, and the soil is rocky so few plants live there. There is a lot of volcanic activity on the islands.

■ Galápagos penguins

Penguins and seals can live in the Galápagos because the currents keep the sea temperature at about 60° F. (15° C.), which is just right for them.

Darwin and the islands

Charles Darwin was a famous scientist. He visited the islands and studied the animals he found there. Darwin developed a theory about how these and all other animals develop over time. We call this process evolution.

▲ **Charles Darwin**

The first finch on the Galápagos

This one eats only plants and grubs.

This one eats grubs off cactus plants.

This finch eats only plants.

▲ In the Galápagos there are finches that have beaks of different lengths. It depends on what foods they eat. But it is believed that they all came from a single species over a long period of time. It is this process of evolution that Darwin set out to explain.

● **To the Parent**

Galápagos is an old Spanish word for the big land tortoise found only in these islands. These turtles are typical of the seemingly prehistoric creatures that inhabit the place. The marine iguana feeds on the species of seaweed that grows only there, so it is unique in the world. Although formidable in appearance the creatures of the Galápagos neither fear nor attack people. It is easy to see how this place inspired Charles Darwin.

? What Is the Mystery of Easter Island?

(ANSWER) Easter Island is far away in the south part of the Pacific Ocean. The island has hundreds of old stone statues. No one knows why these giant statues were built. We also do not know who made them.

▼ **Easter Island statues.** One of the strangest things about them is that every one faces inland, away from the sea. Nearly all of them show only the body from the waist up.

How Were the Statues Made and Set in Place?

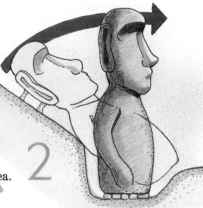

▶ Next the statue was cut away from the rock under it. It was pulled up so it stood in the ditch. The statue faced away from the sea.

▲ How could people with simple tools build such big statues? It was probably done in steps like the ones here. First the builders dug a ditch until they found a big piece of rock. They carved the face right onto this rock.

◀ Gravel and sand were piled behind to hold up the statues. Some of them stood more than 40 feet (12 m) in height.

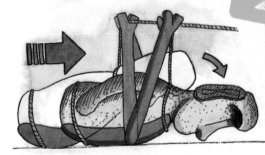

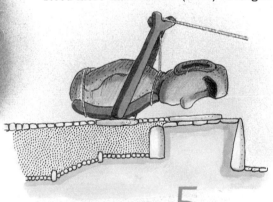

The statue was hauled to the site.

4

Now came one of the hardest steps. The builders had to move the statues. To do this they built a kind of wooden rocker. They placed each statue on the rocker. When people pulled on the ropes attached to it the statue moved like a rocking chair. Each time it rocked the statue moved forward a bit. In this way the statue was pulled slowly along the ground.

▶ When they reached the right spot the statue was turned on the rocker. A special red piece was put on its head.

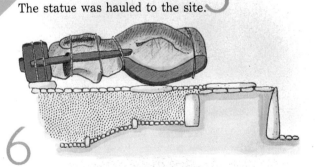

● **To the Parent**

Easter Island got its name from the fact that it was discovered on Easter Day in 1722. It is famous for the huge stone statues and for the ruins of giant stone walls. These statues vary in height from 3 to 40 feet (1 to 12 m). Some believe they depict important people who were deified after they died. But that is conjecture. The ancient inhabitants of the island were captured and enslaved or died from diseases brought to the island by ships.

▶ The statue was slowly pulled up. Dirt and stones were piled to keep it from falling down. Once the statue stood up, the dirt and stones were taken away.

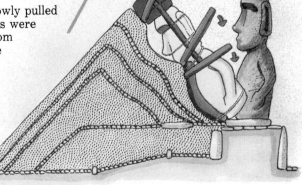

? What Is a Pyramid?

ANSWER The pyramids were built long ago in the country of Egypt. In ancient times Egypt was ruled by leaders called pharaohs. When one of the pharaohs died a giant pyramid was built. This was the pharaoh's grave, or tomb. The people of Egypt believed that someone who died would live again. So they put inside the pyramid things that he would need in his next life.

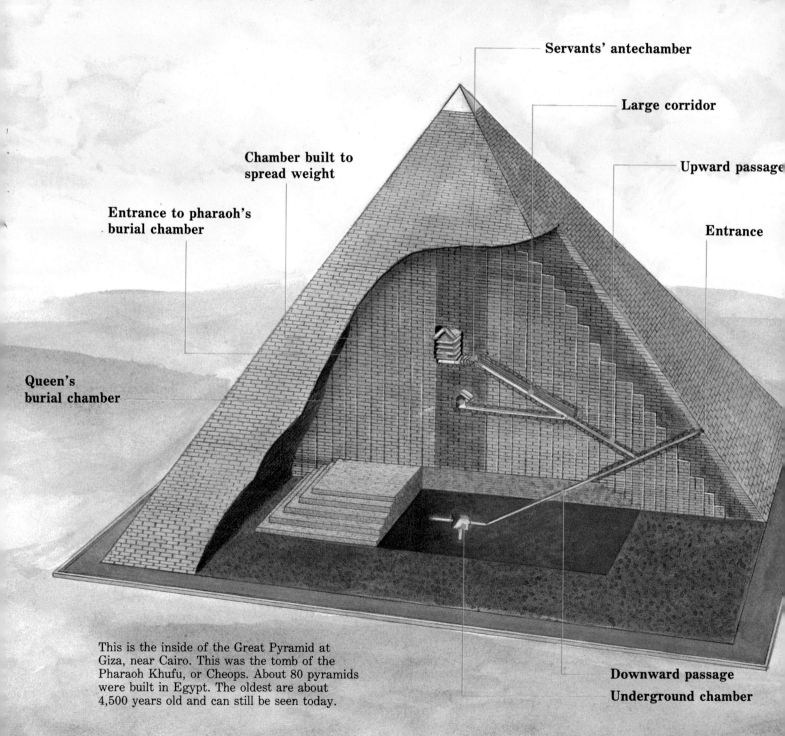

Servants' antechamber

Large corridor

Upward passage

Entrance

Chamber built to spread weight

Entrance to pharaoh's burial chamber

Queen's burial chamber

Downward passage

Underground chamber

This is the inside of the Great Pyramid at Giza, near Cairo. This was the tomb of the Pharaoh Khufu, or Cheops. About 80 pyramids were built in Egypt. The oldest are about 4,500 years old and can still be seen today.

▲ The Sphinx, a make-believe creature with a lion's body and human head, stands guard beside the pyramids.

Mediterranean Sea

Cairo

Giza

Valley
of the Kings

Red Sea

River Nile

■ Early tombs were broken into by grave robbers, so later ones were built in a valley up the Nile from Cairo now called the Valley of the Kings.

Tomb of Queen Hatshepsut

River Nile

Tomb of Thutmose III

Tomb of Seti

Tomb of Ramses II

☐ Tombs
■ Graves

▲ Decorations in a tomb   ▲ Gold mask of Tutankhamen

Great Tombs of the World

Throughout history, in many parts of the world, powerful rulers have ordered that grand tombs be built for themselves.
The great tombs are intended to remind the world of these rulers' greatness.

Pyramid of Pharaoh Khufu

About 482 feet (147 m)

About 755 feet (230 m)

About 2,244 feet (684 m)

Imperial tomb, Japan

115 feet (35 m)

1,594 feet (486 m)

About 984 feet (300 m)

About 1,896 feet (578 m)

Imperial tomb, China
About 164 feet (50 m)

Why Is the Sahara So Famous?

ANSWER The Sahara is the biggest desert in the world. It covers nearly a fourth of the whole African continent. It reaches into 12 countries and stretches 3,500 miles (5,600 km) from east to west and 1,063 miles (1,700 km) north to south.

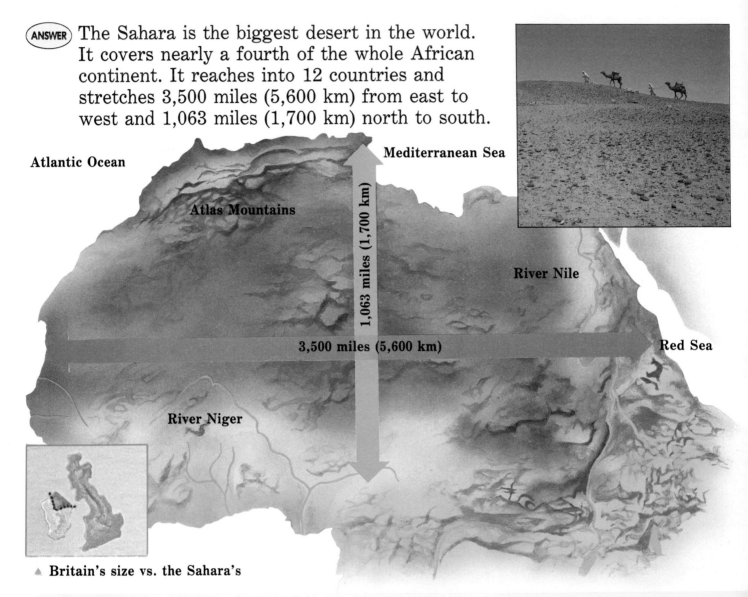

Atlantic Ocean

Mediterranean Sea

Atlas Mountains

1,063 miles (1,700 km)

River Nile

3,500 miles (5,600 km)

Red Sea

River Niger

▲ Britain's size vs. the Sahara's

Animals of the Sahara

Like all deserts the Sahara gets little rain. Because of this very few plants and animals can live there. Those that do have developed special ways to survive in this hot, dry world. They usually live near what little water there is. To be safe from the desert heat, many of these animals sleep all day in holes in the ground. Then they come out at night when it is cooler.

▲ **The horned viper.** It has an odd way of getting to where it wants to go. It makes an S of its body and slithers across the sand sideways.

▲ **The Sahara fox.** In the daytime it keeps cool in a hole tunneled in a sand dune. It comes out only at night, when the hot sun has set.

Why Doesn't the Desert Get More Rainfall?

Most of the world's deserts are found in regions that reach north and south of the equator. Dry air from the desert regions meets damp air coming from around the equator and forms clouds. These clouds drop huge amounts of rain at the point where they are formed. But then when it has lost its moisture the dry air rises, curves all the way around and drops back down to earth over the desert. The dry air has no more water to release on the desert as rain. And this is why deserts are such barren, dry places.

Dry air blows down over the desert

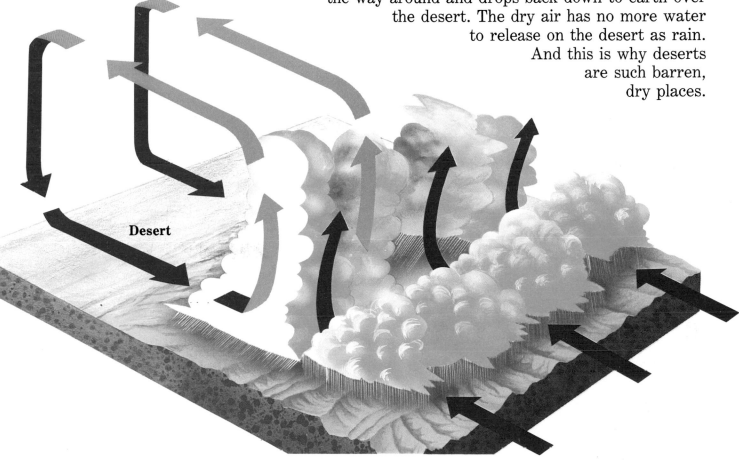

Desert

▲ **The desert scorpion.** In its tail it carries a deadly sting. After the sun has gone down it comes out to capture and kill insects to eat.

▲ **The jerboa.** Also called a jumping rat, it has powerful back legs to help it bound across the sand in leaps of two feet (.6 m) or more.

● **To the Parent**

Sahara is from the Arabic word meaning desert. This desert stretches from the Red Sea to the Atlantic Ocean, and it is larger than the Mediterranean Sea. Its very low rainfall does not encourage the growth of plants, although there are a few. Some animals also live in the desert, although they are primarily small nocturnal ones, and a number of reptiles. The fruit of the date palm, which can ordinarily be found in and around oases, provides a little food for the people who make the desert their home.

❓ What Was the Reason For Building the Aswan High Dam?

 ANSWER Egypt is mostly desert. There is some farmland along the banks of the River Nile. At times in the past, there has been very little water in the river. At other times it rained so much that the river caused floods. To stop this a dam was built upstream at Aswan. In the rainy season it keeps the River Nile from flooding. In the dry season it sends down extra water for the farmers to use.

■ Since ancient times the people of Egypt have had to worry about floods and about not having enough food to eat. The Aswan High Dam has helped to end these problems. Now farmers can grow crops all year round.

■ There is no longer any fear of the Nile flooding.

Now with the dam I don't worry when it rains.

Mediterranean Sea

Suez Canal

Cairo

Suez

River Nile

Sinai Peninsula

Red Sea

Aswan High Dam

| 0 | 50 | 100 Mi |
| 0 | 80 | 161 Km |

■ The dam is also a source of electric power

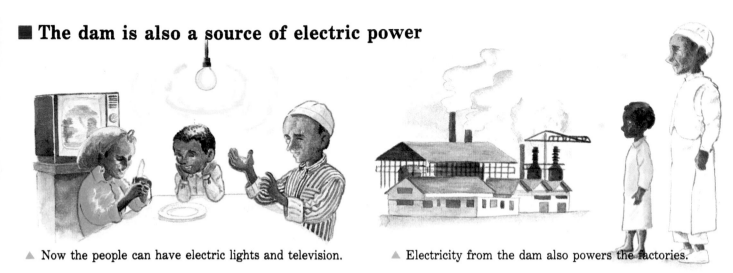

▲ Now the people can have electric lights and television.

▲ Electricity from the dam also powers the factories.

Aswan High Dam

The dam is more than two miles (3.5 km) across, almost a mile (1,300 m) thick and 361 feet (110 m) high.

■ The Nile's water level stays the same

The water level of the River Nile used to change greatly with the change of seasons. Sometimes it would rise 20 feet (6 m) or more between the dry and rainy seasons. Now with the dam controlling the flow the water level stays the same.

❓ What Was the Silk Road?

(ANSWER) The Silk Road was an ancient trail. It linked China and the countries of Europe. Along this path traders carried China's most famous product, silk. They sold it in the markets of Europe. The Silk Road was about 4,000 miles (6,400 km) long. Much of it crossed the desert of the Middle East. The road was one way that people in Europe and Asia learned about each other.

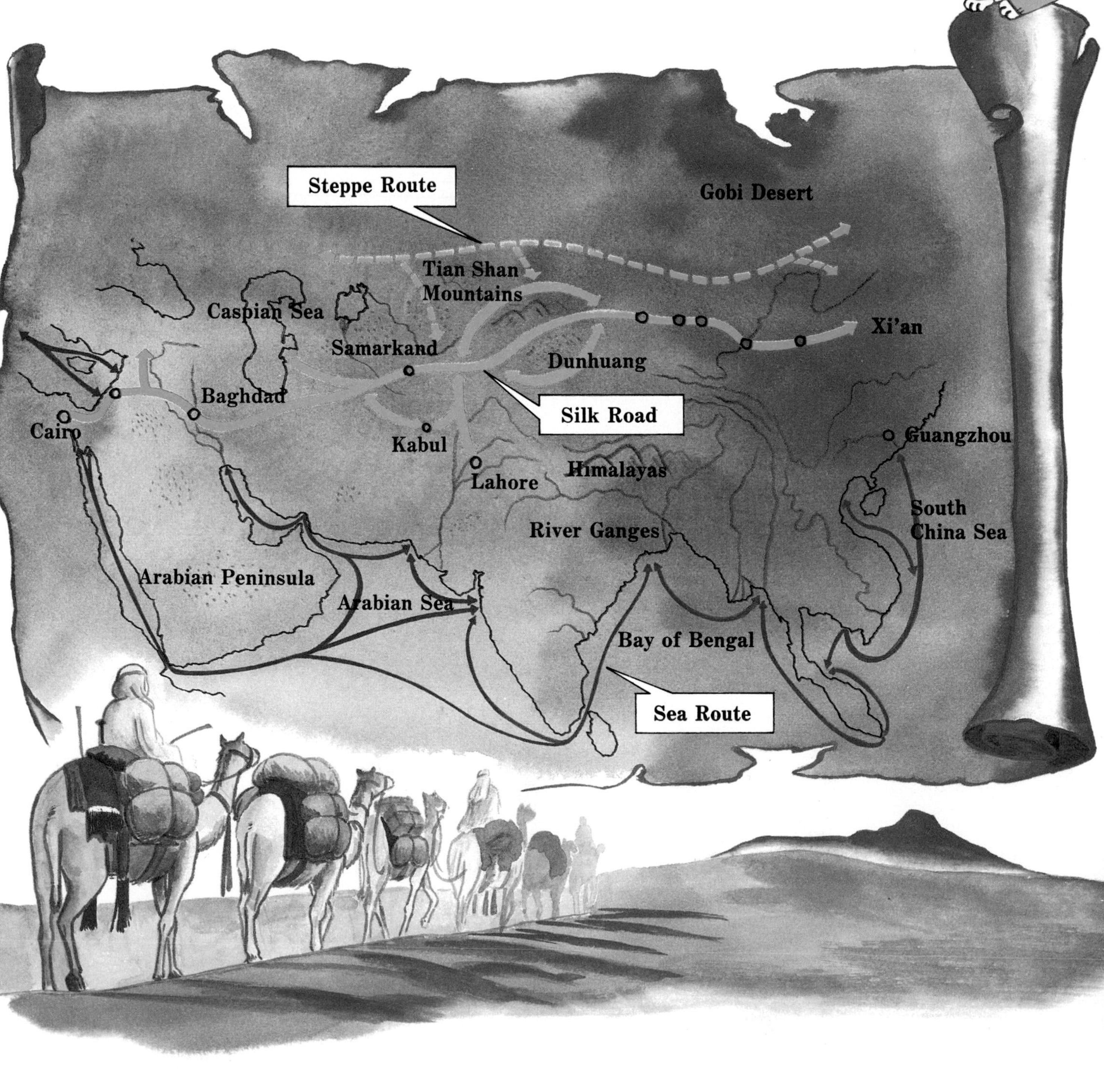

Steppe Route

Gobi Desert

Tian Shan Mountains

Caspian Sea

Samarkand

Baghdad

Dunhuang

Silk Road

Xi'an

Cairo

Kabul

Guangzhou

Lahore

Himalayas

River Ganges

South China Sea

Arabian Peninsula

Arabian Sea

Bay of Bengal

Sea Route

What Else Did They Use the Road For?

In addition to silk, many other products traveled along the road. There were common things like fruits and vegetables. But the road also helped people in different parts of the world learn from one another. For example the way to make paper and to raise silkworms came to Europe along this road.

Silk

Silk making

Paper making

Gunpowder

Pottery making

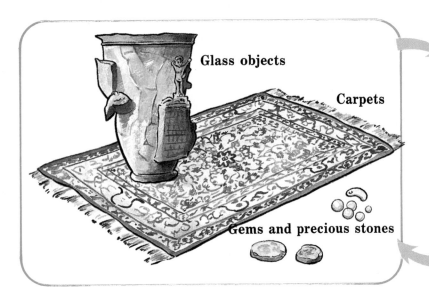

Glass objects

Carpets

Gems and precious stones

What Sorts of Places Were On the Road?

Much of the Silk Road followed trails through the desert. Along the road were many oases. In these towns people and animals could rest. On the edge of one desert in China was the town of Dunhuang. It was one of the most important stops in and out of China. People from all over the world came through there. The town became a place where their ideas and cultures mixed together. As a result of this, beautiful artwork can still be seen in the buildings and caverns of Dunhuang.

● To the Parent

Portions of the Silk Road date back to about 2,000 B.C. Its route has changed with events. In the 6th Century A.D., for example, Mesopotamia was the scene of bitter fighting between the Byzantine Empire and the Sassanid rulers of Persia. To avoid the area caravans began taking a more northerly route, so the older, more central, Silk Road fell into disuse and oases along the way lost business.

▲ These houses are carved into the sides of hills. They are decorated inside with paintings that are very old.

❓ How Were the Himalayas Formed?

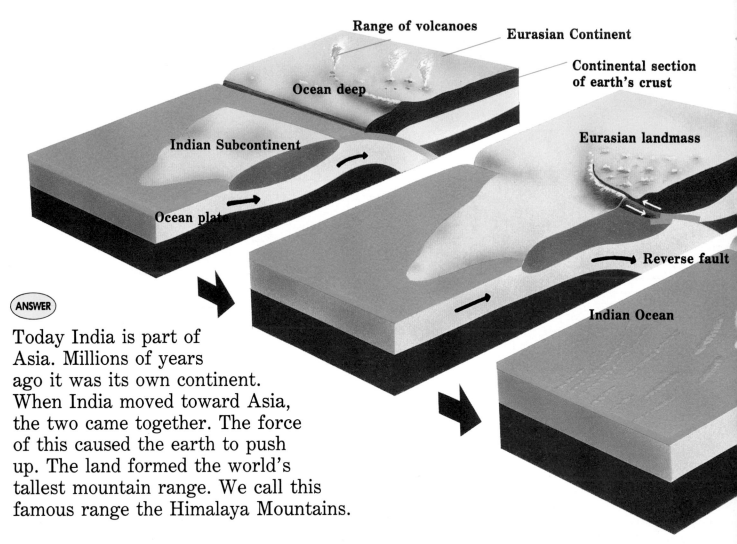

Range of volcanoes

Eurasian Continent

Continental section
of earth's crust

Ocean deep

Indian Subcontinent

Eurasian landmass

Ocean plate

Reverse fault

Indian Ocean

ANSWER

Today India is part of
Asia. Millions of years
ago it was its own continent.
When India moved toward Asia,
the two came together. The force
of this caused the earth to push
up. The land formed the world's
tallest mountain range. We call this
famous range the Himalaya Mountains.

Roof of the World

The Himalayas are the highest mountain range in the world. This mighty chain has 26 peaks of 25,000 feet (7,620 m) or more. British-led climbers in 1953 were the first to conquer the massive Mt. Everest.

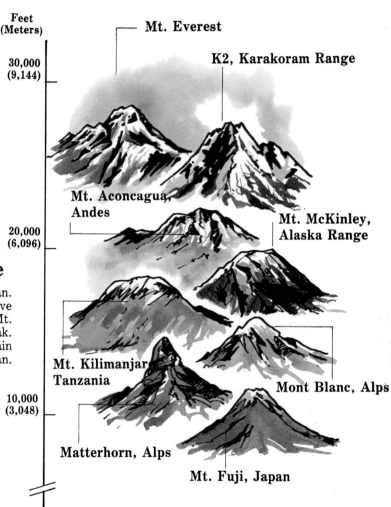

Feet (Meters)

30,000 (9,144)

20,000 (6,096)

10,000 (3,048)

Mt. Everest

K2, Karakoram Range

Mt. Aconcagua, Andes

Mt. McKinley, Alaska Range

Mt. Kilimanjaro, Tanzania

Mont Blanc, Alps

Matterhorn, Alps

Mt. Fuji, Japan

■ Fossil evidence

Shellfish live in the ocean. Yet fossils of shellfish have been found near the summit of Mt. Everest, the world's highest peak. That shows that this mighty mountain pushed up from the floor of the ocean.

Tian Shan Mountains

Plateau of Tibet

Himalayas

▼ Many of the world's highest peaks are here.

● To the Parent

The Himalayas were pushed up when India bumped into the Eurasian landmass millions of years ago. Where the two landmasses collided, there was a wrinkling of the earth's surface, and this is how the world's highest mountain range was formed. It is thought-provoking to reflect that these lofty peaks once formed part of the ocean floor. It provides a concept of the passage of time and the spectacular changes that materialize in our world. Try to imagine what your environs were like millions of years ago.

What Was the Reason For Building the Taj Mahal?

ANSWER This is the Taj Mahal. It was built hundreds of years ago. At the time, Shah Jahan was ruler of India. His wife was Queen Mumtaz Mahal. When she was dying she asked that a beautiful monument be built. This would keep the memory of her name alive. Shah Jahan followed her final wish and built the Taj Mahal. Today it is one of the most famous buildings in the world.

▼ **The Taj Mahal at Agra, India**

■ A sameness

The Taj Mahal was designed so that it looks the same viewed from any direction. Although the peaked dome appears very large from the outside it is even more impressive when seen from inside. It is hollow and rises to a height of nearly 100 feet (30 m) above the surrounding structures.

▼ **Front view**

Hollow space

▼ **Overhead view**

Coffin of Mumtaz Mahal

Coffin of Shah Jahan

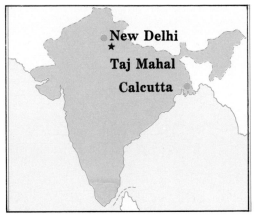

New Delhi
★
Taj Mahal
Calcutta

4 ...she contracts a fever and dies. She was only 36 years old.

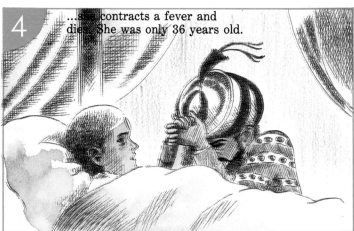

1 Young Shah Jahan meets Mumtaz in the bazaar and falls in love.

5 It is said that Shah Jahan was so saddened by his wife's death that his hair turned white overnight.

2 They marry five years later. He is 20 years old, and she is just 17.

6 In memory of his beloved queen he builds the exquisite Taj Mahal.

3 Mumtaz bears many children, but after the 14th is born...

● To the Parent

Shah Jahan was the fifth ruler of the Mogul Empire. While Taj Mahal is a corruption of his wife's name and the monument is dedicated to her memory, it is believed that he also intended for it to stand as a spiritual focus of the Moslem faith in the empire. Craftsmen from as far away as Persia and the Middle East helped build it. Twenty thousand people worked on the building, which took 22 years to build. Today the beautiful edifice of white marble is considered the perfect example of Mogul architecture, and many also believe it to be the most beautiful building in the world. It endures as a tribute to love and perfection.

?️ How Long Is the Great Wall?

ANSWER The Great Wall stretches from east to west across China. From one end to the other is a distance of 1,500 miles (2,400 km). The real length of the wall, as it snakes up and down hills and around obstructions, is nearly twice that great. It is said to be the only thing built on earth that can be seen from the moon.

▶ China's Great Wall can be seen from the moon.

How long would it take to walk the Great Wall?

If you walked 2½ miles (4 km) an hour night and day, how long would it take to walk the length of the Great Wall? Remember, this winding wall covers about 3,000 miles (4,800 km).

1,500 miles (2,400 km)

The ends of the Great Wall are 1,500 miles (2,400 km) apart. But you would walk 3,000 miles (4,800 km) as it twisted and turned across China. Your hike would take more than seven weeks.

How Did They Build Such a Big Wall?

The Great Wall was built over many years by many thousands of workers.

1 Two huge fences were first built of logs, and then the space in between them was filled in to form the wall.

2 The original wall was built up with layers of packed earth, trees and reeds, and these were left to harden.

3 Much later, in the 16th Century, the outer sides were buttressed with bricks, which have survived till now.

Why Was the Wall Built?

The Great Wall of China was built as a defense against wandering tribes that invaded China from time to time. The wall was first built about the 5th Century B.C. but fell into disrepair. In 221 B.C. the emperor Shi Huang Di had it restored. The wall is built of earth and stone, and its height varies from 20 to 30 feet (6 to 9 m). All along its length tall watchtowers provided a view of the countryside.

Why Are These Hills So Famous?

ANSWER This beautiful scenery can be seen around the Chinese city of Guilin. The hills rise sharply out of the flat plains around them. The tallest hills reach 980 feet (300 m) into the sky. They are well known because they are often seen in the paintings of Chinese artists. The odd shape of the hills is due to erosion. It took thousands of years for the hills to form.

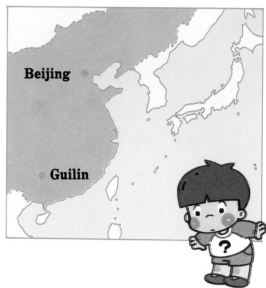

▼ The landscape of Guilin is often seen in Chinese paintings.

How Did the Hills Get Such Unusual Shapes?

Long ago the land here was covered with gently rolling hills. But the plains were made of a very soft rock, called limestone. When rain fell on the plains the rock began to dissolve. As plants grew their roots broke up the ground some more. Rainwater seeped into the ground. The erosion continued below the surface, and underground caverns formed.

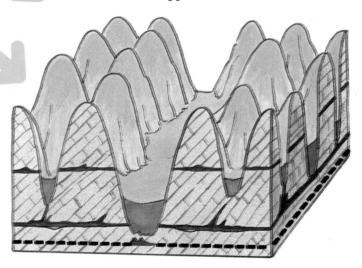

The process of erosion continued. The cracks in the limestone grew wider and deeper. Over time the water level dropped. The caverns dried out.

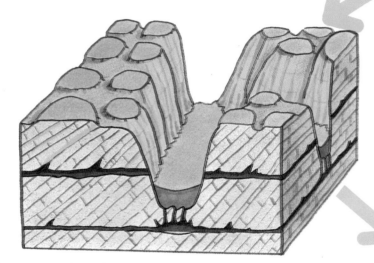

Above the ground the erosion continued for thousands of years. The shape of the hills became steeper, until they looked like they do today. Beneath many of the hills of Guilin you can find the caverns that helped to form them.

■ Stalactite caves

Stalactite caves are a feature of limestone areas. Stalactites are formed when rainwater seeps through limestone, absorbing some of the lime. As the water drips off the ceilings of underground caverns it leaves lime deposits, which hang from the roof like icicles. These are called stalactites.

▲ **Stalactite cave at Guilin**

● **To the Parent**

Guilin's peaks are a favorite theme in the paintings of the southern school of Chinese art. Typically the mist-shrouded mountains are depicted towering behind a lake or river upon which floats a sampan, or boat. The effect is quite enchanting, and a great many people assume that it is a figment of the artist's imagination. But such scenery actually exists in the Guilin region. The unusual landscape here results from the effect of an extremely hot, humid climate on the limestone bedrock. Pillars of limestone rising almost straight upward the way those at Guilin do are found only in areas that are tropical or subtropical.

What Is the Longest Undersea Tunnel in the World?

ANSWER That is the Seikan Tunnel, which runs between the Japanese islands of Honshu and Hokkaido. It is 33 miles (53 km) long and is a railroad tunnel. There is a railway platform right inside the tunnel so that the passengers can get off the train and take a look around.

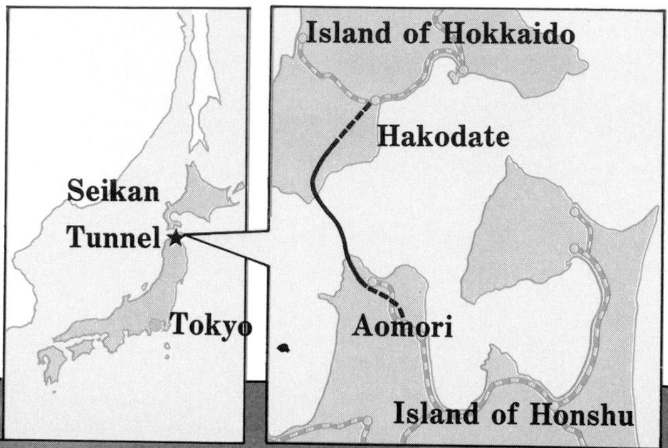

Island of Hokkaido

Hakodate

Seikan Tunnel ★

Tokyo

Aomori

Island of Honshu

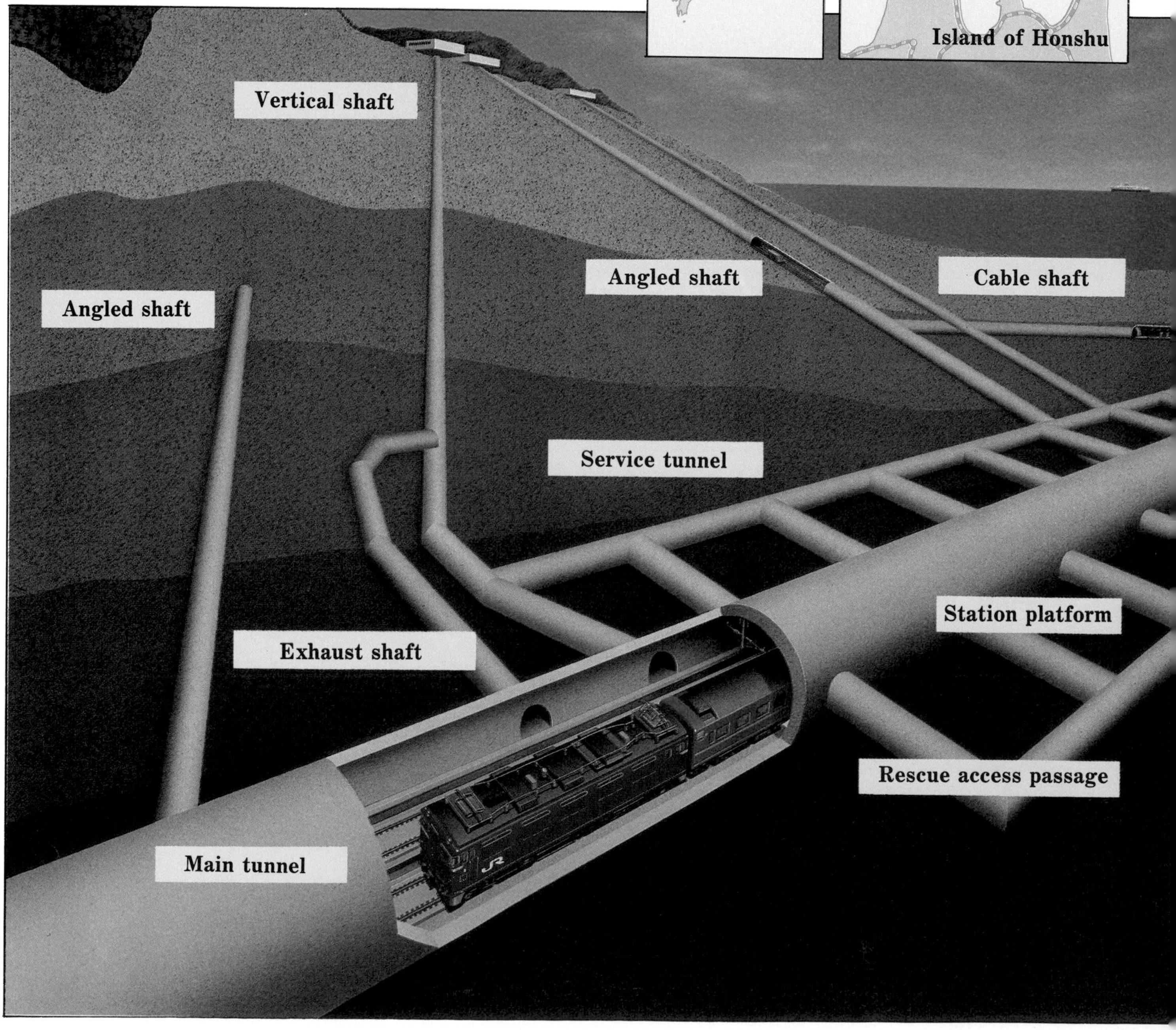

Vertical shaft

Angled shaft

Angled shaft

Cable shaft

Service tunnel

Station platform

Exhaust shaft

Rescue access passage

Main tunnel

■ A cross section

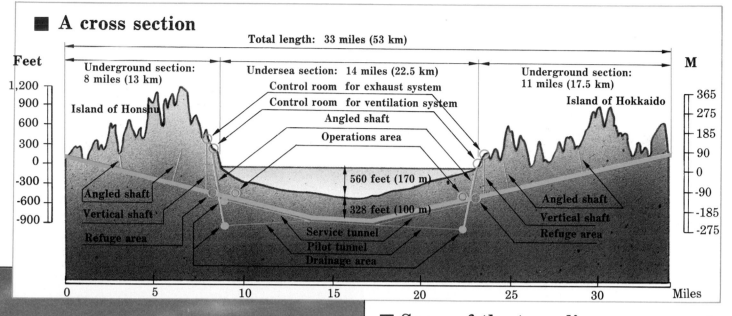

Total length: 33 miles (53 km)

Feet | M

Underground section:
8 miles (13 km)

Undersea section: 14 miles (22.5 km)
Control room for exhaust system
Control room for ventilation system
Angled shaft
Operations area

Underground section:
11 miles (17.5 km)

Island of Honshu

Island of Hokkaido

1,200
900
600
300
0
-300
-600
-900

365
275
185
90
0
-90
-185
-275

560 feet (170 m)

328 feet (100 m)

Angled shaft
Vertical shaft
Refuge area

Angled shaft
Vertical shaft
Refuge area

Service tunnel
Pilot tunnel
Drainage area

0   5   10   15   20   25   30   Miles

Fire tunnel

Pilot tunnel

▲ There is a passenger platform in the tunnel.

■ Some of the tunnel's measurements

The Seikan Tunnel is large. It is nearly 26 feet (7.9 m) high and about 32 feet (9.8 m) across. The seamless railway track used in the tunnel is 32.6 miles (52.5 km) long. The tunnel is fitted with the very finest safety and rescue equipment.

▼ **Equipment**

Lighting

Sprinkler

26 feet (7.9 m)

Passages for escape

32 feet (9.8 m)

Sprinkler

● **To the Parent**

Starting with geological surveys in 1946, construction of the Seikan Tunnel took 42 years. Counting all the service and emergency escape tunnels there are a total of 18 tunnels with a length of 44.6 miles (71.8 km). The railway track through the tunnel is the longest seamless track in the world. A station platform beneath the sea is the only such station to be found anywhere. State-of-the-art safety and rescue equipment, including laser measuring devices, was installed in the tunnel.

Did You Know That in Australia There's a Rock Two Miles Long?

ANSWER Ayers Rock is a single huge rock. It rises out of a desert area in the center of the Australian continent. It is the largest single rock anywhere in the world.

▼ Ayers Rock

■ How high is this rock?

Ayers Rock reaches a height of about 1,150 feet (350 m) above ground. The distance around it is about 6 miles (10 km). Ayers Rock stands higher than Paris's Eiffel Tower and is many times the size of the Great Pyramid in Egypt. It is a popular tourist attraction.

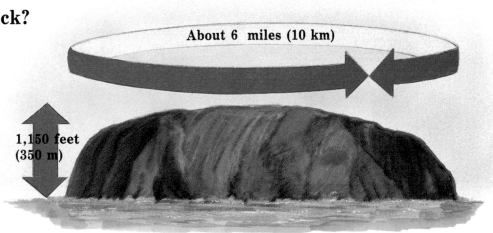

About 6 miles (10 km)

1,150 feet (350 m)

How Was Such a Rock Formed?

In the center of Australia there is little rainfall and the air currents are unusual. For more than 600 million years, dry winds wore away this rocky land. Over time the land gradually turned into desert. However, some rock was harder than the rest and did not wear down. This is why some scientists think an enormous rock shaped like a loaf was left standing almost at the exact center of the Australian continent.

Air currents. The winds ▶ of the region seem to circle around Ayers Rock.

Before erosion began long ago this region was a flat plain.

Wind erosion gets under way, but one part of the area is unchanged.

Erosion continues and eventually forms what we now call Ayers Rock.

Does Australia Have Other Odd Land Formations?

Yes, it does. Wind and rain carved strange rock shapes in this region of Australia. They have been given names, like Devil's Marbles, Kangaroo Tail and Wave Rock, that describe the way they look.

▼ **Devil's Marbles**

Wave Rock ▶

● **To the Parent**

With few external influences reaching the continent in the millions of years before modern times, Australia has been able to preserve many extraordinary examples of the work and artistry of nature. Since the first rocks were formed approximately four billion years ago the landscape of this isolated continent has undergone few major changes. For this reason Australia has been called the Land Where Time Stands Still. But weathering by sun and wind has eroded the land, creating some unusual and beautiful works of art.

❓ What Is So Special About Australia's Great Barrier Reef?

ANSWER It is the largest reef in the world. It stretches for about 1,250 miles (2,000 km) along Australia's coast. The Great Barrier Reef is made from the skeletons of billions of tiny creatures called coral. They live in colonies hundreds of years old.

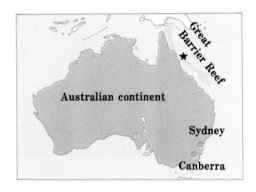

Great Barrier Reef

Australian continent

Sydney

Canberra

▲ The reef is an actual coastal barrier.

How Did This Coral Reef Take Shape?

The ocean must be about 70° F. (21° C.) with adequate sunlight for coral to survive. So they live close to the surface.

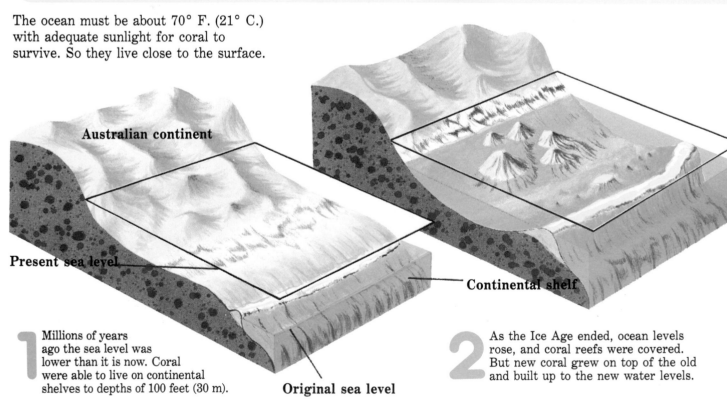

Australian continent

Present sea level

Continental shelf

Original sea level

1 Millions of years ago the sea level was lower than it is now. Coral were able to live on continental shelves to depths of 100 feet (30 m).

2 As the Ice Age ended, ocean levels rose, and coral reefs were covered. But new coral grew on top of the old and built up to the new water levels.

More than 350 kinds of coral live on the reef. ▶

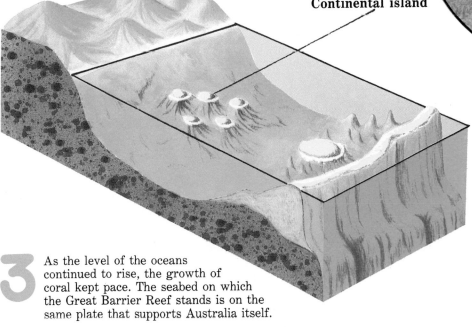

Continental island

3 As the level of the oceans continued to rise, the growth of coral kept pace. The seabed on which the Great Barrier Reef stands is on the same plate that supports Australia itself.

❓ What Kind of Place Is Antarctica?

(ANSWER) Antarctica is the land of the South Pole. It is one of the continents, only slightly smaller than South America. It is the coldest place on earth. Even in summer the temperature never goes above -20° F. (-29° C.). Many nations have research bases there, but Antarctica is not owned by any nation.

Antarctica as seen from space ▶

▲ Penguins are the best-known inhabitants of Antarctica. Most species of them live only in Antarctica.

■ How thick is the ice there?

Almost all of Antarctica is covered by a thick cap of ice.
Its average thickness is about 5,900 feet (1,798 m).

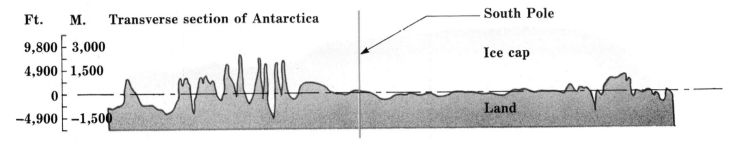

Ft.	M.	Transverse section of Antarctica
9,800	3,000	
4,900	1,500	
0	0	
−4,900	−1,500	

South Pole

Ice cap

Land

■ Days without nights

In December and January the
sun never sets in the Antarctic.
This photograph shows how the
sun moves but does not set.
There are 24 hours of daylight.

■ Aurora

The aurora is a beautiful
light that can be seen
over the North and South
Poles. Over Antarctica
it is sometimes known
as the southern lights.

■ The animals of Antarctica

Penguins, seals and sea gulls are some of
the animals that live on the continent.

◀ Seals   ▲ Penguins

● To the Parent

In contrast to the Arctic, which
is merely a huge pack of ice with
no land beneath it, Antarctica is
an enormous ice-covered continent.
The presence of this continent was
confirmed in 1820. After that a
race developed between explorers
from many nations to reach the
South Pole. A team from Norway,
led by Roald Amundsen, was the
first to succeed when it arrived
at the pole on December 14, 1911.

❓ What Are These?

■ Cologne Cathedral

This is a picture of Cologne Cathedral in West Germany. It is one of the most famous churches in Europe. People began working on it in the year 1248. Work continued on and off for centuries. It took more than 600 years to build. Its two steeples are 515 feet (157 m) tall. The building is longer than one and a half football fields. Cologne Cathedral was badly damaged during World War II. But after the war it was carefully repaired.

■ Westminster Abbey

This is Westminster Abbey. This church in London is one of the most famous places in all of Great Britain. A church has stood on this spot for more than 1,000 years. For the past 800 years nearly all the kings and queens of England received their crowns here. When they die the rulers of England are buried at the Abbey with many other important citizens.

■ Fontainebleau Palace

This palace is located in a small town outside the city of Paris, France. It sits at the edge of a beautiful forest. In the past there was a hunting lodge here that was used by the kings of France. More than 400 years ago the lodge was rebuilt and turned into a royal palace. Today Fontainebleau Palace is a public museum.

■ Schönbrunn Palace

This beautiful palace is in the country of Austria. It is located in the capital city of Vienna. There are more than 1,400 rooms in the palace. Visitors come here to see the palace and the lovely gardens and trees all around it. The palace was one of the homes of the family that ruled Austria.

■ The Matterhorn

This is a mountain in the famous range called the Alps. The Matterhorn sits on the border between the countries of Italy and Switzerland. It is not among the tallest mountains in the world. But the steep peak of the Matterhorn presents a great challenge to mountain climbers.

■ The White House

Everybody knows the famous American who lives here. The White House is the home of the President of the United States. It is located in Washington, D.C., at 1600 Pennsylvania Avenue. There are more than 130 rooms and offices in the President's home. He lives with his family on the second floor.

● **To the Parent**

There are impressive buildings, beautiful landscapes and places of special historical importance in every corner of the globe. Each holds a story. Share these stories with your child and it will make learning more enjoyable for him or her. It will also provide your child with a greater awareness of other people, other places.

? And These?

■ Temples of Abu Simbel

These temples are in Egypt. They were built in ancient times. The temples were carved out of stone on the bank of the River Nile. When the Aswan High Dam was built it was feared that water would destroy the temples of Abu Simbel. To save them they were moved to a new location.

■ Sydney Opera House

The Sydney Opera House has become Australia's most famous building. Its unusual design makes it immediately recognizable. The building took 16 years to construct, cost $102 million and was opened by Britain's Queen Elizabeth II in 1973. There are four performance halls.

■ Temple Of the Emerald Buddha

This temple is located in the country of Thailand. The people there call it Wat Phra Keo. Inside is a statue of Buddha that is special to the Thai people. Some of the clothes on this statue are made of real gold.

Growing-Up Album

Where Are These Famous Places?

Can you name the countries where you will find the places shown in the drawings on these pages? Look at the map of the world and try to spot them. If you don't know, don't be afraid to guess.

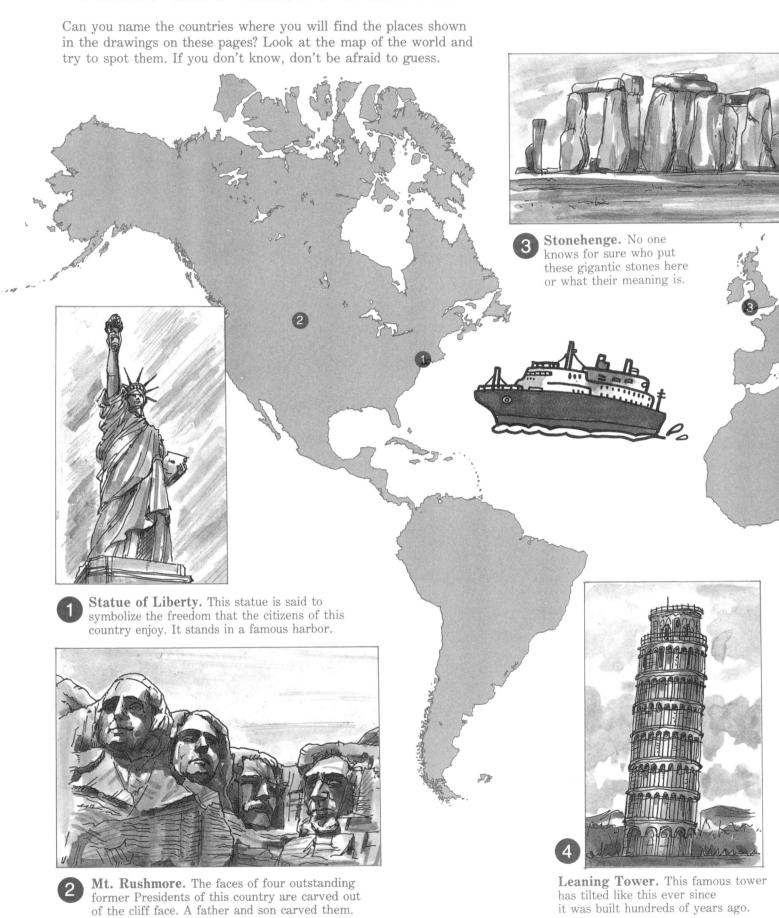

3 Stonehenge. No one knows for sure who put these gigantic stones here or what their meaning is.

1 Statue of Liberty. This statue is said to symbolize the freedom that the citizens of this country enjoy. It stands in a famous harbor.

2 Mt. Rushmore. The faces of four outstanding former Presidents of this country are carved out of the cliff face. A father and son carved them.

Leaning Tower. This famous tower has tilted like this ever since it was built hundreds of years ago.

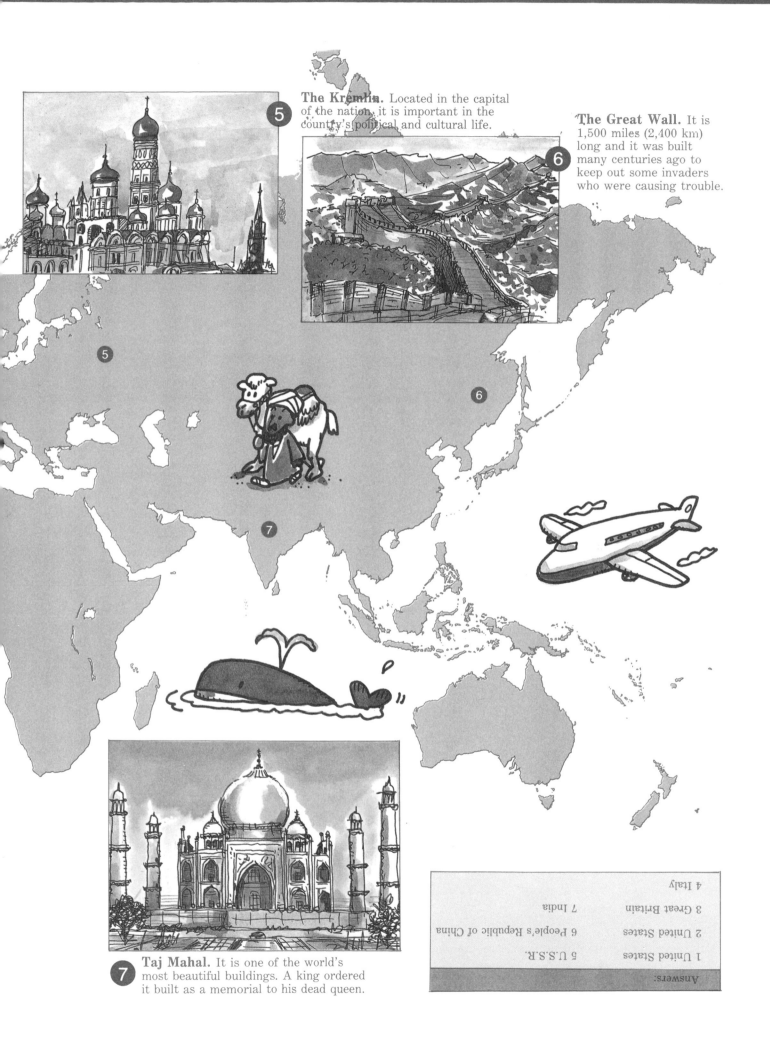

The Kremlin. Located in the capital of the nation, it is important in the country's political and cultural life.

The Great Wall. It is 1,500 miles (2,400 km) long and it was built many centuries ago to keep out some invaders who were causing trouble.

Taj Mahal. It is one of the world's most beautiful buildings. A king ordered it built as a memorial to his dead queen.

Have You Ever Seen These Before?

Look at the illustrations on these pages. If you have ever been to any of these countries and seen these things for yourself put a check by them. If you have read about them in another book or seen them on television put a double check. If you read about them in this book put three checks.

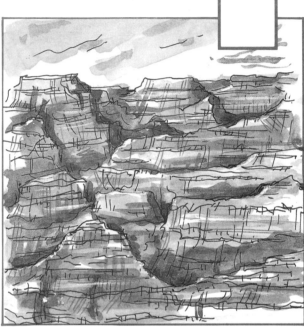

Grand Canyon. This enormous deep gorge was cut by the Colorado River. It is in Arizona.

Windmills in Holland. Windmills were used in the past to pump water and to mill grain by harnessing the power of the wind. They provided free energy.

The Pyramids. Built using huge stone blocks long, long ago, they were the tombs of Egypt's pharaohs.

Niagara Falls. This most famous waterfall of all is on the border between the United States and Canada.

Eiffel Tower. This is the world-famous landmark of Paris. More than 1,000 feet (300 m) high, it dominates the skyline.

Ayers Rock. Located almost in the center of Australia, it is the biggest single rock found in the world. It is almost flat on top.

The Colosseum. Men fought for their lives in this arena.

Tower Bridge. It spans the River Thames and is one of London's famed landmarks.

The Parthenon. This is what remains of a great temple which was dedicated to a goddess of ancient Greece.

Match the Words and Pictures

Look at the descriptions of famous places numbered 1-8
and match them to the correct illustration. Write the
correct number in the space provided beside the description.

1 Vatican City

2 Sahara

3 Venice

4 Antarctica

These are long, deep inlets formed
by glaciers thousands of years ago
along the coasts of Northern Europe.

The longest undersea tunnel in the
world, it connects two islands of
Japan. It took 42 years to build.

This is a shortcut between the
Atlantic and Pacific Oceans for
ships. It is in Central America.

The smallest country in the world,
it is surrounded by the city of
Rome. It has many famous paintings.

⑤ Easter Island

⑦ Seikan Tunnel

⑥ Panama Canal

⑧ Scandinavian fjord

This Italian city is famous for its many canals and its gondolas. Once it was an important trading center.

This huge region in Africa is covered entirely by sand. Rain seldom falls, and not many animals can survive here.

This place is famous for its many huge stone statues. No one is sure how or why they happen to be there.

This is the southernmost part of the world. It is covered with snow and ice. Many penguins live there.

A Child's First Library of Learning

Famous Places

TIME
LIFE ®

Time-Life Books Inc. is a wholly owned subsidiary of
The Time Inc. Book Company.
Time-Life Books, Alexandria, Virginia
Children's Publishing

Publisher:	Robert H. Smith
Managing Editor:	Neil Kagan
Associate Editor:	Jean Burke Crawford
Marketing Director:	Ruth P. Stevens
Promotion Director:	Kathleen B. Tresnak
Associate Promotion Director:	Jane B. Welihozkiy
Production Manager:	Prudence G. Harris
Editorial Consultants:	Jacqueline A. Ball
	Andrew Gutelle

Editorial Supervision by:
International Editorial Services Inc.
Tokyo, Japan

Editor:	C. E. Berry
Associate Editor:	Winston S. Priest
Writer:	James H. Shaw
Translation:	Pauline Bush
Editorial Assistant:	Nobuko Abe

Library of Congress Cataloging in Publication Data
Famous places.
    p.   cm. — (A Child's first library of learning)
    Summary: Answers questions about such marvels as the
Pyramids, Taj Mahal, Grand Canyon, and Stonehenge,
describing how they were made and what makes them great. An
activities section is included.
    1. Geography—Miscellanea—Juvenile literature.
[1. Geography—Miscellanea. 2. Questions and answers]
I. Time-Life Books.   II. Series.
G133.F33 1989   910'.76   89-20405
ISBN 0-8094-4893-9
ISBN 0-8094-4894-7 (lib. bdg.)
©1989 Time-Life Books Inc.
©1988 Gakken Co. Ltd.

Second printing 1991. Printed in U.S.A.
Published simultaneously in Canada.

TIME-LIFE is a trademark of Time Warner Inc. U.S.A.

Time-Life Books Inc. offers a wide range of fine publications,
including home video products. For subscription information, call
1-800-621-7026 or write TIME-LIFE BOOKS, P.O. Box C-32068,
Richmond, Virginia 23261-2068.